ONE DAY IN MY LIFE

One Day in My Life

BOBBY SANDS

INTRODUCTION
by
SEAN MacBRIDE, S.C.

THE MERCIER PRESS
DUBLIN and CORK

The Mercier Press Limited
4 Bridge Street, Cork
24 Lower Abbey Street, Dublin 1

© The Bobby Sands Trust, 1982

ISBN 0 85342 682 1

First published January 1983
Reprinted March 1983
Reprinted May 1984

Printed in the Republic of Ireland

Contents

Biographical Note on Seán MacBride, S.C.

President International Peace Bureau (Geneva); President NGO Committee (Geneva); Member International Commission of Jurists; Hon. President World Federation United Nations Associations; President Irish United Nations Association; President Irish Section Amnesty International.

Mr MacBride who was one of the founder members of Amnesty International was Chairman of its International Executive for thirteen years, was Secretary-General of the International Commission of Jurists for seven years, and was President of the International Commission for the Study of Communications Problems (1977-1980); he was Assistant Secretary-General of the United Nations and Commissioner for Namibia (1973-1976); Mr MacBride has acted as a member of several International Commissions of Enquiry.

He is the holder of the Irish Military Medal (1920-1921); Noble Prize for Peace (1974); the International Lenin Prize for Peace (1977); the American Medal of Justice (1978); Medal of the International Institute for Human Rights (1978); UNESCO Medal of Merit (1980); Dag Hammerskjoeld Award (1981).

The following honorary degrees have been awarded to Mr MacBride: Doctor of Letters (D.Litt.), Bradford University (1977); Doctor of Laws (LL.D.), Saint Thomas, Minnesota (1975); Doctor of Laws, Guelph University, Canada (1977); Doctor of Laws, University of Dublin (1978); Doctor of Laws, University of Cape Coast, Ghana (1978); Doctor of Laws, Florida Southern College (1979); Doctor of Laws, Suffolk University, Boston (1980).

Introduction

by

Seán MacBride, S.C.

O Wise Men, riddle me this:
What if the dream come true?
What if the dream come true?
And if millions unborn shall dwell
In the house that I shaped in my heart,
The noble house of my thought? . . .
Was it folly or grace?
Not men shall judge me, but God.

PÁDRAIG MAC PIARAIS

The pages that follow are a human tale of suffering, determination, anguish, courage and faith. They also portray frightening examples of man's inhumanity to man. They make sincere, but harsh reading.

Why then publish them? Is it really necessary to read them? It is to the answer to these two questions that I propose to address myself in this introduction.

The reaction to the hunger-strike and the death of Bobby Sands and his comrades* has been varied and contradictory. To the British establishment which rules that portion of our country known as Northern Ireland it appeared a victory in a contest of wills

---

* Francis Hughes, died 12 May 1981; Raymond McCreesh and Patsy O'Hara died 21 May 1981; Joe McDonnell died 8 July 1981; Martin Hurson died 13 July 1981; Kevin Lynch died 1 August 1981; Kieran Doherty TD died 3 August 1981; Thomas McElwee died 8 August 1981; Michael Devine died 20 August 1981.

between 'Irish terrorists' and a strong-willed British prime minister: 'By God, we have taught them a lesson! They will now know that we mean what we say. We have broken their morale!' To the IRA and their supporters it was a triumph of endurance and courage. If proof were needed, it was evidence of their determination to pursue unflinchingly their campaign of violence until British forces and administration were withdrawn from Northern Ireland. It was a morale booster for their cause. A cause that depended more on integrity and courage than on what politicians and lawyers term 'reason and common sense'.

To the bulk of the Irish people it was a tragedy that tore asunder the strings of their heart and their conscience. Many of them disagreed with the methods used even though they had sympathy for the objectives that the men of violence were seeking to achieve.

There were also some Irish people who through some perverted form of intellectual snobism had become hostile to the concept of a united and free Ireland; there were others too who, for reasons of personal advancement, still hankered after the trappings of British influence in Ireland. These were comparatively few and indeed did not include the majority of those who had given allegiance to the former pro-Treaty party. Be it said in fairness to the Fine Gael rank and file that probably the majority of them are by now supportive of a united Ireland and were sympathetic to Bobby Sands. Fianna Fáil was clearly sympathetic; so were the Labour supporters with the exception of two or three anti-national mavericks.

Centuries of oppression, bribery and duplicity have led to a certain ambivalence in a section of our people: this is best described as 'the slave mentality', or the 'gombeen' psychosis. This makes it difficult to assess the real sentiment of some of our people on certain issues.

The majority of the ordinary decent people of England are not really interested in what happens in Ireland. Their knowledge of Anglo-Irish relations is minimal. They have been taught to regard the Irish people as impossible and irrational, even if somewhat amusing and gifted. They could not care less as to what is happening in Ireland. They are oblivious to the fact that the partition of Ireland has been created, imposed and fostered by the British establishment. They have been led to believe that the British presence in Northern Ireland is essential in order to prevent 'those impossible Irish from killing each other'. They conceive their role as that of an honest broker who is keeping the peace in this turbulent island. They ignore, and do not particularly wish to know of, the grievous sufferings which have been inflicted on the Irish people in the course of the British conquest and occupation of Ireland. Whenever this is mentioned, they just complain that our memories are too long and that we should forget the past.

They are not aware, or do not admit to being aware, of the brutal repression and injustices from which Ireland suffered right up to the Treaty of 1921. They are not aware that the settlement which they imposed on the Irish people under threat of 'immediate and terrible war' in 1921 caused a Civil War in Ireland which lasted for several years and which prevented any normal political development. They are not aware that the enforced partition of Ireland has resulted in a virtual state of continuous civil war, both in Northern Ireland and in the Republic, since 1922.

The reality, however, is that the partition of Ireland by Britain in defiance of the will of the overwhelming majority of the Irish people has disrupted the life of Ireland — North and South — for over sixty years. It has cost thousands of Irish — and indeed British — lives. Irish jails have been continually filled to bursting point. Several hundred thousand Irish men and women have passed through Irish and English jails over the last sixty years because of partition. The normal application of the rule of law has been disrupted since 1922 in both parts of the country. The Statute Books contain every conceivable form of coercive and repressive legislation. The normal protection of human rights under the law is subject to so many exceptions and qualifications that we cannot adhere to the international standard without constant derogation.

Worse still, successive Irish governments have been placed in the absolutely false position of attempting to justify and defend partition. It is upon the Irish governments that the task of manning and sealing an impossible border which is unacceptable to the majority of the Irish people falls. The army and the police have to be constantly augmented in order to maintain this unwanted border. This puts Irish governments, opposed as they are to partition, in an increasingly difficult position *vis-à-vis* their own constituencies as they have to jail and oppress their own young people in order to protect British rule in the north-east corner of our island. The subversive organisations naturally trade on this situation and are able to obtain the support of the younger generation. Thus the cycles of violence and repression continue to escalate; this weakens the authority of the government, the courts and the police. The financial implications resulting from this situation are incalculable; it has been said, probably correctly, that the cost of partition to the Irish government in terms of increased security measures, prisons, special courts, compensation, extra police and military, amounts to twenty per cent of the total state expenditure.

There are a number of responsible persons in England who do appreciate Britain's responsibility in trying to correct the workings of history. One such person is a leading Anglican theologian Dr John Austin Baker,* who was the chaplain to the Speaker of the British House of Commons. During the hunger-strike in a sermon in Westminister Abbey, on 1 December 1980, he pointed out:

No British government ought ever to forget that this perilous moment, like many before it, is the outworking of a history for which our country is primarily

---

* The Right Reverend Dr John Austin Baker who was a distinguished lecturer in theology at Oxford, and was rector of St Margaret's, Westminster, has now been elevated to the rank of Bishop of Salisbury.

responsible. England seized Ireland for its own milit-
ary benefit; it planted Protestant settlers there to make
it strategically secure; it humiliated and penalised the
native Irish and their Catholic religion. And then,
when it could no longer hold on to the whole island,
kept back part to be a home for the settlers' descen-
dants, a non-viable solution from which Protestants
have suffered as much as anyone.

Our injustice created the situation; and by con-
stantly repeating that we will maintain it so long as the
majority wish it, we actively inhibit Protestant and
Catholic from working out a new future together. This
is the root of violence, and the reason why the protes-
ters think of themselves as political offenders.

In Northern Ireland itself, the ordinary laws were
abrogated and a police-state regime was installed.
Because the British authorities and those who sup-
ported British rule in Northern Ireland feared that the
nationalist minority, would increase more rapidly
than the pro-British population, which was generally
Protestant, a regime of wholesale discrimination was
installed. The reason for installing a draconian system
of discrimination, based on religious beliefs, was that
by preventing Catholics from obtaining employment
or housing, their numbers could be kept down. They
would not be able to get married and they would not
be able to obtain employment. This would force them
to leave the area, thus ensuring that the Catholic
population would decrease.

A new generation of young people, however, resented the discrimination that was being implemented
to their detriment. They could get neither employ-

ment nor housing. All employment and promotion within all services was strictly reserved to non-Catholics. Notices were displayed outside factories proclaiming: 'No Catholics employed here'.

Gradually, as was inevitable, the rising generation of young people resented a situation in which they were treated as third class citizens and were precluded from obtaining employment or housing. They became dissatisfied and disillusioned with existing political parties in the North as well as in the South and they started a perfectly legal and constitutional civil rights campaign demanding an end to the discrimination which prevailed and insisting on their civil and political rights. They obtained the support of the majority of the nationalist population in the North, and indeed, the active support and sympathy of the population in the rest of the country. Bernadette Devlin McAliskey became one of their leaders and swept aside the existing more moderate politicians. The rise of this new Civil Rights Movement was met with violent repression by the British forces and the police. Their members were arrested, interned and subjected to systematic police harassment. Their meetings were broken up by the police. This culminated in the killing of thirteen civilians by British soldiers at a perfectly legal public demonstration on 30 January 1972, now known as Bloody Sunday, in Derry city.

These acts of oppression by the British forces had two results. In the first place they solidified and increased the support for the Civil Rights Movement, and on the other hand, they influenced the young

13

people to turn more and more towards the IRA and physical force. The IRA availed of this situation to become the defenders of the Catholic population against the attacks of the police and the British military forces. The methods used by the British forces became more and more indefensible. Prisoners were systematically tortured by means of sophisticated methods imported from England. This was fully exposed and condemned in the course of legal proceedings brought by the Irish government before the European Commission of Human Rights in Strasbourg and assurances were given by the British government that these methods would be discontinued. It is claimed by the IRA that these methods have not been discontinued, but are now being applied more secretly.

As the extent and nature of the oppression grew, so did the IRA reaction to it, and we have had a constant escalation in what is now a full-blown guerrilla war, in the course of which some 628 members of the British forces have been killed and 7,496 wounded in the period 1969–June 1981. In the same period, 1,496 civilians were killed and 16,402 wounded. The total number of persons killed in this small area over the last ten years is 2,124, and the number wounded is 23,898. There are at present in Northern Ireland 1,244 republican prisoners. These are variously described by the British authorities as terrorists or criminals; by the nationalist population they are regarded as political or republican prisoners.

As a result of this situation there were on 11 June

1981 1,244 male prisoners serving sentences in British prisons in Northern Ireland for what the British describe as terrorist type offences. In addition, there were on the same date approximately 50 women prisoners also serving sentences. It must be borne in mind that none of these prisoners were convicted after trial in due process of law. They were tried by single-judge courts without any juries. These courts are known as 'Diplock' courts. These are courts which follow procedures that do not conform with those applicable to normal trials under the rule of law. Of some 1,300 prisoners serving sentences in British jails in Northern Ireland, 328 have been receiving what the prison authorities describe as 'special status treatment'. The balance of some 966 have been denied this 'special status treatment' because they were convicted on a date subsequent to the withdrawal by the British authorities of the 'special status treatment'. In effect, what the hunger-strikers in the H-Blocks at Long Kesh were demanding was that they should receive special status treatment. This had been spelled out by the hunger-strikers and the other prisoners in five specific demands concerning:

1. The right to wear their own clothes at all times.
2. The prisoners requested that they should not be required to do menial prison work; they were prepared to do all the work required for the maintenance and cleaning of the portions of the prison occupied by them. They also asked that study time should be taken into account in determining the amount of work which they were required to do.

3. They requested the right to associate freely at recreation time with other political prisoners.

4. They requested the right to a weekly visit, letter or parcel, as well as the right to organise their own educational and recreational pursuits in the prison.

5. The right to remission of sentences as is normally provided for all other prisoners.

The prisoners believed that the refusal of the British authorities to grant them the 'special category status' which obtained in regard to other prisoners was a political decision taken in order to criminalise their status. Several hundred of them went on what is called 'the blanket protest', from September 1976. This protest consisted of refusing to wear prison clothes and wearing a blanket instead. As from March 1978 they escalated their protest to a 'no-wash protest'. A number of them went on hunger-strike in October 1980 and the hunger-strike ended on 18 December 1980 on the basis of an agreement put forward by Cardinal Tomás Ó Fiaich and Bishop Daly. In the course of the negotiations between Cardinal Ó Fiaich and Bishop Daly, the British government had agreed substantially to the demands made by the prisoners provided that they were not described as 'an acceptance of political status'. This proviso was accepted by the prisoners. However, the British government failed to implement the recommendations that had been made by Cardinal Ó Fiaich and substantially accepted by them. This caused considerable bitterness and distrust among the prisoners. They considered that they had been tricked into giving up the hunger-strike by subterfuge in which the British government availed of the good offices of Cardinal Ó Fiaich, but then reneged on the agreement they had made with him.

Cardinal Ó Fiaich and Bishop Daly also considered that they had been misled by the British government. It is in this atmosphere that the later hunger-strike was started on 1 March 1981. However, on this occasion, the prisoners started the hunger-strike with the pre-conceived determination that they were not going to allow the British government to trick them again, or to use intermediaries; they insisted that they would continue the hunger-strike until death in relays until such time as the British government gave categorical assurance to them concerning the future treatment of prisoners, and the granting of the five requirements which they had specified.

In the meanwhile, a succession of well-intentioned intermediaries including a number of members of the Irish parliament, representatives of the European Commission on Human Rights, representatives of the Irish Commission on Justice and Peace and representatives of the International Committee of the Red Cross sought to mediate but the attitude of the British government throughout had been:

We cannot accept that · mediation between the government and convicted prisoners, even by international bodies of the highest standards is the right course.

They also refused to negotiate directly with the prisoners. In reality, the attitude of the British government had been to avail of all the intermediaries in an effort to break the determination of the prisoners and to avoid negotiating with the prisoners thus not binding themselves to alterations in the prison rules. The prisoners accused them of playing a cynical game of brinkmanship, waiting for one prisoner after the other to reach the dying point, hoping that this would break the morale of the other prisoners. Indeed, in the course of a press interview given by Mr Michael Alison, British minister of state for Northern Ireland in the British embassy in Washington, he made the startling but candid admission that negotiations about the hunger-strikers was like:

> the efforts of authorities to keep plane hijackers occupied while plans are developed to subdue them. (Irish Times 13 July 1981)

The death of Bobby Sands and his writings are but a fall-out resulting from the cruel interference by Britain in the affairs of the Irish nation. I wish it were possible to ensure that those in charge of formulating British policy in Ireland would read these pages. They might begin to understand the deep injuries which British policy has inflicted upon this nation, and now seek to heal these deep wounds.

As was pointed out by the Taoiseach Charles Haughey, 'For over sixty years partition has not worked, and it is not likely to work now.' Why not face up to this situation now without any further strains on Anglo-Irish relations?

No one in Ireland would wish to impose any discrimination or injustice upon any minority, religious or political, that may exist in any portion of Ireland. In a united federal Ireland I am sure that special guarantees could be ensured that would protect any religious minority that felt threatened. I am sure that, within the context of the European Convention for the Protection of Human Rights and Fundamental Freedoms, special mechanisms could be instituted to ensure the administrative and judicial protection of any minority within the Federated Republic of Ireland.

However, such a solution will only become possible when Britain finally relinquishes any claim of sovereignty over any portion of this island. The withdrawal of British forces can, if necessary, be phased over a period of years. More important, and more urgent, would be the immediate cessation of overt and covert British secret service operations in any part of Ireland; these are now commonplace, and are a grave source of danger. Such secret service operations can only aggravate the situation and cause an added complication in the already difficult relations which exist between our two islands.

Lest this introduction by me to these harrowing pages be construed as a tacit endorsement of violence I should explain my attitude. I do not agree with violence. Throughout the hunger-strikes I did not participate in any of the H-Block Committee activities lest this might be construed as an approval of violence. This was a difficult decision for me to make as I was only too conscious of the provocation and intolerance which was a feature of the policy of the British authorities *vis-à-vis* the hunger-strike. I did make my views known to the British authorities in no uncertain terms but did not do so publicly. Because of persistent misrepresentation of the facts involved in the hunger-strike by the British authorities in the United States I did make one speech in New York under the auspices of the American Irish Unity Committee on 22 July 1981 in order to set the record right.

In their own country and in countries which they do not seek to dominate, the British are reasonable, fairminded and even lovable. It is otherwise in areas which they regard as their preserve. In regard to Ireland the British government and establishment are just incapable of being objective, fair-minded or just. A typical illustration of this was provided recently.

The British forces in Northern Ireland have been using rubber or plastic bullets indiscrimately for a number of years. They have argued that they were harmless. Over fifty people — mostly children — have been killed or permanently maimed in Northern Ireland by these plastic or rubber bullets. This was denied by the British who maintained that they were harmless. When extensive riots broke out recently in Britain the possibility arose of using rubber or plastic bullets for crowd control. An alarmed Conservative British Home Secretary said immediately that he would oppose their use 'in mainland Britain because they are lethal!' *(Irish Times, 11 July 1981)* It is all right to use them in Ireland and to kill women and children there — but not 'in mainland Britain!'

In the early stages of the last decade, Paul Johnson, one of Great Britain's most distinguished journalists, editor of the *Spectator*, and one of Prime Minister Margaret Thatcher's most ardent supporters, wrote in *The New Statesman*:

> *In Ireland over the centuries, we have tried every possible formula: direct rule, indirect rule, genocide, apartheid, puppet parliaments, real parliaments, martial law, civil law, colonisation, land reform, partition. Nothing has worked. The only solution we have not tried is absolute and unconditional withdrawal.*

Why not try it now? It will happen in any event!

> *Some had no thought of victory*
> *But had gone out to die*
> *That Ireland's mind be greater*
> *Her heart mount up on high;*
> *And yet who knows what's yet to come.*
> *W. B. YEATS*

SEAN MacBRIDE, 1982

21

Publisher's Note

Robert Sands, M.P., spent four and a half years in the H-Blocks of Long Kesh concentration camp outside Belfast. He did not spend all of this time in any one block. From time to time he was moved around to various parts of the prison. He went on hunger-strike on 1 March 1981 and died sixty-six days later on 5 May 1981.

He wrote the present work on sheets of toilet paper with biro refills in a small filthy cell covered with excrement. It was not all written at the one time which explains a certain unevenness in the style and content. The written sheets were smuggled out over a period of time. The text and handwriting have been authenticated by the Sands' family and the contents corroborated by other prisoners.

Certain sections of the original manuscript have been omitted from this book on legal advice. Otherwise only minor textual changes for the sake of consistency and clarity have been made.

It should be pointed out that the British and Northern Ireland authorities have denied that there were any beatings or torture in Long Kesh. But they have taken no effective steps to refute the masses of published material in books and journals alleging the existence of such torture, particularly in a book published in 1979 called *The H-Blocks* by two responsible clergymen, Rev. Fathers Faul and Murray in which scores of signed and witnessed statements from prisoners concerning their ill-treatment were published. This book had a massive circulation and is still in print.

Royalties accruing from the sale of *One Day in My Life* are paid to a Bobby Sands Trust Fund set up for the benefit of the wives, families and dependents of prisoners.

One Day in My Life

It was still dark and snowing lightly when I woke. I don't think I got more than an hour's sleep during the long restless torturous night. The cold was intense, biting at my naked body. For at least the thousandth time I rolled over on to my side, hugging the blankets close to my body. The sleep that the bitter cold had denied me, hung above me, leaving me tired and drowsy. I was somewhat exhausted, and every bone in my body seemed to be protesting at the ordeal of having spent yet another night on a damp foam mattress on the floor. No sleep again worth mentioning! I was frustrated, cross and curled up in a little ball to get warm. If I had had something to boot, I would have booted it, that's just how I felt. I had tried lying in every sort of position to get warm, but the cold still penetrated. My three flimsy blankets were no match for the bitter, biting cold that came creeping through the bars of my window, situated above my head.

Dear God, another day I thought, and it was a far from pleasant thought. Naked, I rose and crossed the cell floor through the shadows to the corner to urinate. It was deadly cold. The stench rose to remind me of my situation and the floor was damp and gooey in places. Piles of rubbish lay scattered about the cell and in the dimness dark, eerie figures screamed at me from the surrounding, dirty, mutilated walls. The stench of excreta and urine was heavy and lingering. I lifted the small water container from amongst the rubbish and challenged an early morning drink in a vain effort to remove the foul taste in my throat. God it was cold.

It was beginning to grey outside as dawn approached, and the crows began to assemble themselves in long black lines upon the snow-covered barbed wire fencing. One morning I am going to wake up out of this nightmare, I thought, as I huddled in under the blankets again. Apart from the caws of the crows it was sinisterly quiet. I was sure many of the lads lay awake, probably just lying huddled up trying to get warm. The prospect of cold, tasteless porridge along with two slices of bread and half a mug of lukewarm tea for breakfast was depressing. It was simply demoralising just thinking of it.

The dawn broke and out of the shadows of the dead night materialised the daily nightmare. The dirt and filth, the scarred walls — the inner confines of my stinking, smelly tomb greeted me once again. I lay listening to my own gentle breathing and to the caws of the crows.

The snow lay deep upon the outside yard. Didn't I know it only too well, having spent half the night huddled up in the corner while it fell in through the bars of my window to its earthly destination upon my bed. In the first light of morning boredom began to set in. The day ahead would seem like eternity and depression would soon be my companion again. I lay there, freezing cold and uncomfortable, feeling a bit sorry for myself with the thought of yet another day churning around in my head.

A key clinked against the steel. Footsteps came charging along the outside corridor breaking the silence. The crows fled in an explosion of chattering caws; my mind fought to register the meaning of the disturbing confusion. Panic gripped me as the heavy steel door rattled and flew open. A wave of black uniforms swept into my cell blotting out the door space. A gruff, intimidating voice yelled, 'Right you, get up!'

I was already half way to my feet before the last syllable left his rowdy mouth, wrapping my threadbare old blue towel around my shivering waist.

'Bears in the air' echoed throughout the wing as those awake and alerted by the invasion warned the rest of the lads that there were screws in the wing.

'Wing shift,' someone shouted, leaving me in no doubt as to what was to come.

'Right you, out and up to the top of the wing and be quick,' rowdy mouth snapped. I moved out of the cell, the corridor was black with uniforms, batons dangling by their sides.

'Not quick enough,' rowdy mouth snapped again.

Two strong pairs of arms gripped me from behind. My arms were wrenched up my back and my feet left the floor. A mass of black thronged around me and moved in a sudden burst of speed dragging me along with it. I came back to earth and a well-polished pair of leather official issue boots ground into my feet. A screw on the perimeter of the now excited gang kneed me in the thigh. I felt like vomiting and screaming surrender but I remained mute. A table loomed up before me where half a dozen or so screws converged, gaping and inspecting me — their first intentional prey. I was left standing in the midst of the black horde who awaited their cue from the mouthpiece.

'Right,' screamed the self-appointed tyrant. 'Drop that towel, turn round. Bend down and touch your toes.'

I dropped my towel, turned a full circle and stood there embarrassed and naked, all eyes scrutinising my body.

'You forgot something,' the mouthpiece grunted.

'No I didn't,' I stammered in a fit of bravado.

'Bend down tramp,' he hissed right into my face in a voice that hinted of a strained patience. Here it comes, I thought.

'I'm not bending,' I said.

Roars of forced laughter reinforced by a barrage of jibes and abuse erupted.

'Not bending!' the confident bastard jibed.

'Not bending! Ha! Ha! He's not bending, lads,' he said to the impatient audience.

Jesus, here it comes. He stepped beside me, still laughing and hit me. Within a few seconds, in the midst of the white flashes, I fell to the floor as blows rained upon me from every conceivable angle. I was dragged back up again to my feet and thrown like a side of bacon, face downwards on the table. Searching hands pulled at my arms and legs, spreading me like a pelt of leather. Someone had my head pulled back by the hair while some pervert began probing and poking my anus.

It was great fun; everybody was killing themselves laughing, except me, while all the time a barrage of punches rained down on my naked body. I was writhing in pain. They gripped me tighter as each blow found its destination. My face was smashed against the table and blood smeared the table under my face. I was dazed and hurt. Then they dragged me off the table and let me drop to the floor. My first reaction was to wrap the towel which lay beside me around my reddened waist. Again I was gripped by the arms from behind and dragged towards the other wing. I just caught a glimpse of one of my comrades being beaten and dragged to the table, while in the background someone else was being kicked out of his cell. A cell door opened and I was flung inside. The door slammed shut and I lay on the concrete floor, chest pounding and every nerve in my body strained. Could have been worse, I tried to tell myself as a consolation. But this didn't convince me or my aching body one bit.

The cold drove me off the floor. Every part of my body protested as I made the slow ascent to my feet. A trickle of blood ran from my mouth on to my long shaggy beard and dripped on to the floor. My skin was finely emblazoned with a host of bruises and marks. I was trembling. I hadn't really had very much time to be frightened; everything had moved too fast. Thank God I had not been asleep when they came.

'We'll get those bastards someday,' I told myself. We'll see how big they are then, I thought, as I spat out a mouthful of blood into the corner.

'We'll see how great they are then.'

I began pacing the floor. The cold streamed in through the open window and still clad in only a towel, I really felt it. God I was sore.

More bodies were dragged down the wing.

The bastards were shouting their sadistic heads off, revelling in the blood and pain, all of it ours, of course. God only knows how long it will be before they decide to throw us in a blanket. An empty freezing cold cell, an aching black-and-blue frozen body, a bunch of psychopaths beating men to pulp outside the door and it isn't even bloody well breakfast time yet!

'Suffering Jesus, can it get any worse?' I asked myself, and then answered, 'you know bloody well that it will.' That's what was worrying me.

Regardless of my aching body, I continued to pace the floor trying to get some sort of warmth into my body. My feet were now blue with the cold and I thought my entire body was going to give up to the freezing cold. The shock had worn off and the pain and cold were attacking me relentlessly. The snow had begun falling again. On the outside wire there wasn't a crow to be seen.

A few of my comrades shared their experiences and injuries out the windows of a few cells down the wing. I heard the rattle of the trolley and I knew breakfast was coming, and still no blankets or mattress. Don't forget to see which screws are on the wing today, when the door opens, I reminded myself. We could do with a few quiet screws after this morning's episode, I thought, as the cell door opened and two orderlies with sneers on their freshly washed faces planted the morning offering right into my hands — mug of tea in one hand and a bowl of porridge with two slices of bread lying on top of it in my other hand. A little rat-faced figure with a black hat poked his head round the open door he was leaning against and wearing a smirk said, 'Good morning! Would you care to put on the prison clothing and go to work, clean your cell, wash yourself or polish my boots? . . .

'You wouldn't! Ah well, we'll see after!'

The door slammed shut.

'Bastard,' I said, retreating to the corner to inspect the second catastrophe of the day — the breakfast. I salvaged whatever dry bit of bread I could, and having fished the two slices from the soggy porridge I threw the remainder, porridge and all, against the far wall. Disgusted, I literally forced the meagre bit of bread and lukewarm tea into me. It was bitter cold, so cold that in between sips of tea I had to keep pacing the floor. I thought of the three screws who had stood outside the door while I received my breakfast. Warders 'A—', 'B—' and 'C—'. That was all I needed. Three out-and-out torture-mongers and they'd be here all day. Bloody marvellous, I thought.

The screw who had just spoken to me was 'A—'. He was heartless, sly and intelligent when it came to torturing naked men. There was no physical stuff from him. All purely psychological attacks and cunning tricks. He was a right-out-of-Belsen type, and like the majority of the screws he took great pleasure in attacking the dignity of the naked Prisoners-of-War. He was on a constant ego trip, but then weren't they all once they donned their little black suits with the shining buttons, and were handed their baton and pistol?

The second screw that I had seen was 'B—', a sectarian bigot. He was of medium build, black hair, good looking and all go. He was also an alcoholic and handy with his baton, especially on the younger lads, and that was a regular practice of his.

The remaining screw, and perhaps the worst of the three, was 'C—'. He hated us more than 'B—' the bigot, and he constantly went out of his way to prove it. He never smiled, never spoke unless to make a derogatory remark or hurl abuse. He carried an extra large chip on his shoulder, which we had to bear.

Three perfect bastards, I thought, and I cursed the cold, my aching body and the pangs of hunger that never left me. I continued on my journey to nowhere as I circled the cell floor like a guinea pig, stopping here and there for a moment or two to identify the scratched names on the door and walls; the simple testimony and reminder that others had been and still were in my position. A certain quality of pride seemed to attach itself to the scrawled names of the tortured writers. They were entitled to be proud, I thought, as I moved off to read the scribbled Gaelic phrases and words, noting the progress of the other wings in the Gaelic classes.

'Gaelic classes,' I said it again. I sounded rather odd. But then it was odd, considering that it meant standing at the cell door listening to your mate, the teacher, shouting the lesson for the day at the top of his voice from the other end of the wing when the screws happened to be away for their dinner or tea.

I walked on. The biting cold refused to yield. If I didn't get a blanket or two soon I'd be in trouble. You don't ask for them either. I learned that a long time ago. Show one sign of weakness and you've dug your own grave. Besides, there were forty-three of my comrades in the wing in exactly the same predicament as myself. So forget the moaning and get some heat into your body, I thought, rebuking myself for dangerously playing with thoughts of self-pity and thinking too long and too much of the hardships. It breeds depression and depression is worse than the cold and my aching body put together. My thoughts turned to food. Friday, fish for dinner. Cold potatoes and hard peas. But there was always that vague hope that it might be served hot and with salt on it. I don't know why, because it never was. Maybe it was just something to look forward to like winning the pools or the Irish Sweepstakes. More chance of winning the pools, I admitted to myself. Wasn't it all just living from one stinking cold meal to the next, creating false hope for oneself, clinging to every rumour that came your way? *Scéal, Scéal, Scéal!* The Irish word for news or story that was now so worn out that even the screws used it.

'Have you any *scéal?*'
'Did you hear any *scéal?*'
'The *scéal* is bad, or heavy or fantastic.'

33

It was perfectly understandable. You had to have something to hope for, to look forward to, to speculate on or to cling to. The way a good bit of *scéal* could liven up the wing was unbelievable. Like after the Coalisland to Dungannon march when one of the lads brought back an estimate of the turn-out, plus a smuggled photograph. I nearly cried myself and I'm sure more than a few of the lads did. I'll never forget it, sitting in the midst of a living nightmare without even a friendly face in sight and when it came to my turn to see the picture I looked at it and I never felt so happy in all my life. I just stared at it, and stared at it, never wanting to let go of it. Aren't they grand people, I thought. I felt proud to be fighting for them. It brings a lump to my throat even thinking of it now. Ah, dear God, if it wasn't so cold and if I wasn't so sore I could maybe sing a wee song or two to pass the time. But I'm in no mood or form at all for it.

Nobody at the windows talking. Too busy pacing the floor and licking their wounds.

'Bear in the air,' someone shouted, warning that there was a screw in the wing outside the cells. That was the call we used when someone detected the jingle of a key, the squeak of a boot or a passing shadow. All warned of a hovering screw. I squeezed up close to the door and put my eye to a little chip in the concrete where the door met the wall. I'd noticed it earlier and, as I hoped, it afforded me a restricted but welcome view of a few yards of space on the outside corridor. I caught a glimpse of the shadow first, then the familiar form of 'A—'. He had a few letters and a few packets of tissues in his hand.

'Screw giving out letters,' I yelled in Gaelic at the top of my voice out the door to ease the strained, alerted nerves. 'A—' jumped a little, my voice startling him as it broke the sinister silence. But he carried on with what he was doing. It was normal to shout if anyone knew what was going on. It let everyone else know. There was nothing as nerve-wracking or as frightening as sitting naked behind a closed door not knowing what was going on when danger was lurking and in our predicament danger was constantly lurking.

The screws didn't like Gaelic being shouted about the wing or its use in conversations. It alienated them, made them feel foreign and even embarrassed them. They didn't know what was being said. They suspected that every word was about them and they weren't too far wrong!

I began my journey to nowhere again. As I turned by the window a key hit metal. A shiver swept through me as the lock shuddered and my door opened. 'A—' stood there clutching a couple of packets of tissues and some letters.

'I've a parcel for you,' he drawled in his hateful accent, staring at me, wearing his dominant 'I'm better than you' look.

Some parcel, I thought. A couple of packets of Kleenex tissues.

'You're lucky; you are the only one who got a parcel today,' he said.

Jesus! I felt like vomiting. This was 'A—', the

psychologist at work. Reading me like a book, he said, 'Why don't you put on the prison clothes then you can have some privileges.'

I felt like telling him what to do with his stinking privileges and his parcel for that matter but the tissues would come in handy for standing on on the cold floor.

Keep your head. Bobby, I told myself as he handed me a Parker pen to sign the large book for the parcel. He was loving it all: making it seem as if I was signing a million pound contract for three lousy packets of tissues. He had a letter for me as well. I'd spotted that long ago but he was waiting for me to ask him for it. I didn't. I ignored it. He replaced his expensive pen in his top pocket, grinned and made some comment about the smell of my unwashed body and the stinking evil stench of my cell. He turned to close the heavy steel cell door. 'Oh,' he said, 'I've a letter for you.' He handed it to me. I took it from him and cradled it like a new born child. The door slammed. I pressed my eye against the small hole to see if he was going up to his office at the top of the wing. He was. I yelled in Gaelic again, 'Bear off the air' to let the boys know and retreated to the corner feeling like a new man with my prized possessions — a letter and three packets of tissues! I spread the tissues about the floor and stood on them. They felt like luxurious carpeting compared with the naked concrete. I slid the price-less, several times read and censored, pages of my letter out of the already opened envelope. The letter was scarred with black censored lines here and there, but not as bad as last month's I thought. I immediately identified the familiar handwriting as my mother's. Old faithful, never lets me down! I began reading.

My dear son,

I hope you received my last letter all right. I've been very worried about you and your comrades. Is it cold there, son? I know that you have only three blankets and I read in the Irish News *that many of you have severe 'flu. Keep yourself well wrapped up as best you can, son. I'll say a wee prayer for you all.*

Your sister Marcella had a birthday party for Kevin some time ago. He was one year old. He is a lovely child. You haven't seen him yet son, have you? Your father and brother were asking for you, and so was Bernadette and Mr and Mrs Rooney. I was down at the march on Sunday and there was

████████████████████████████

████████████████████████████

████████████████████ (Censored! The Bastards! I cursed them.) *Everything is going well, son. Maybe it won't be long now.*

The Brits raided the house twice last week and smashed my new Celtic harp that the boys in the Cages sent to me at Christmas. I don't think the Brits are very pleased at the minute son, with all the ████

████████████████████████████

████████████████████████████

their heads must be turned son.

Your brother Seán was down in Killarney and there's slogans painted on all the roads and walls about ███████████████████████████████

███████████████████████████████

███████████████

(H-Block!! you Bastards, I said to myself.)

Well son, I must finish off. It's started snowing. I hope you are all right. We are all behind you, son. I had the child up in the house on Sunday. He says he is going to be a Volunteer when he grows up and get you out of that terrible place. God help him. I'll be up with your father and Marcella on your next visit on the 12th. Well son, God bless you all. I'll see you soon. We all miss you.

Your loving Mother.

God bless her, I said.

Visit today!

'Yahoo!'

'You all right in there, Bobby?'

'All right, Seán. Just remembered I have a visit today. Forgot all about it after that bloody massacre this morning,' I said to my next-door neighbour.

'How did you get on yourself, Seán?' I shouted back.

'I think my nose is broken, Bobby. What about yourself?'

'Not too bad, Seán. The usual — plenty of bruises and a few cuts. Here, I got a letter. I think there were plenty of bombs and a big turn-out at the parade. It was all censored as usual, but I'll find out today on my visit. I'm away to walk, Seán; have to get warm. It's really cold, comrade. Keep your heart up. I'll give you a shout later.'

Yahoo! Visit today. Where are those bloody blankets? I'm freezing to death.

I might see the wee lad today. I haven't seen him in almost nine months. It's the health risk. I'm taking a chance seeing him anytime, I thought, but I just have to see him again. The thought of the stringent body searches I would have to face just to receive a solitary monthly half-hour visit was demoralising.

'Bears in the air! Bears in the air!'

I was at the door like a flash, eye to the small hole. Nothing! I couldn't see a thing. I heard them but I couldn't see them.

'Turnover! Turnover!'

Jesus, cell searches! There's nothing in the bloody cells to search. We'd got a right turning over this morning.

A lock on someone's door shot. I caught a glimpse of 'B—' and 'C—' entering a cell facing me. It was Pee Wee's cell. I heard 'C—' yelling, but I couldn't make out what he was saying. The words were barely audible, but I heard 'B—' screaming, 'Bend over, you little cunt!'

Jesus, they were doing a body search on Pee Wee. Barely turned eighteen and they were forcibly bending him to probe his anal passage. I heard the all-too-common dull thud of blows striking Pee Wee's naked body.

'B—' and 'C—' came swaggering out of the cell like two gun-slingers, smiling.

'Stinking bastards!' Seán screamed out of his cell

door at them.

'Mr "A—", a van for the Punishment Block, please. Pee Wee O'Donnell just assaulted Mr "C—",' said 'B—' giggling.

Must be bad, I thought. He must be bloody bad when they are sending him to the boards to charge him. All part of the cover up. Accuse them and you have another charge of false allegations. War criminals! I said to myself. They're a stinking, dirty shower of war criminals, every last one of them.

They took Pee Wee out of his cell. I caught a glimpse of his small harmless figure. His face was red with blood. His right eye was swollen and his nose gushing blood.

They'll forcibly bath him and cut his hair on the boards. In other words they'll batter him to pulp for the third time today!

The wing was deadly quiet. It was very tense, but the evil atmosphere never left and the tension never lifted.

We'll get you 'C—', I said to myself. We'll get you. And I never meant anything so much in my life.

I was shivering, but I stood at my post at the little accidental spy-hole in case they decided to come back and try the same on someone else. I heard them laughing and boasting in their office of how they had beaten Pee Wee up. Word of what had occurred was filtering down the line to the wing O/C. 'B—' was rattling a bucket and shouting to 'C—' about carrying out a slop out. He made sure we all heard it. They'd come around with the bucket and enter the cells kicking the contents of the filthy chamber-pots about the floor. We couldn't empty them out the windows or doors until late at night. But I knew 'B—' was playing on the already strained nerves of the lads. 'A—' was in charge. He might not risk it. The boys were really angry after what happened to Pee Wee. There would be more trouble. Besides the bedding wasn't in the cells to soak yet. As I was thinking of the bedding and the torturing cold the orderlies came down the wing pushing a trolley carrying our mattresses and blankets.

'Blankets on the air!' I yelled in Gaelic to let the boys know. The cells erupted in a melée of shouts, yells and cheers. The doors began opening and after what seemed like an eternity with the cold apparently growing more intense, my cell door finally opened and the orderlies threw my three flimsy blankets and filthy mutilated mattress upon the floor.

'C—' gave me his dirty 'I hate-your-guts' look and slammed the door. And I hate your stinking guts too, 'C—', I said to myself and dived at the blankets. I wrapped one around my waist and drooped one over my shoulders poncho-fashion, putting the towel around my head and neck like a scarf. I pushed the filthy damp foam rubber mattress in along the wall and sat down on it, wrapping the third and last blanket around my feet. I was like something last seen in Stalag 18 or Dachau. And to tell the truth I felt like it too. My beard became irritated by the towel and the horse hair blankets irked my aching body. It was cold and one of the boys commented out his window that it was snowing again. It could snow in on top of me like last night and the night before. I wasn't moving. I wonder how Pee Wee is? Probably near dead in those Punishment Blocks. Jesus, it's been a bad day, I thought and I felt very tired. The exhaustion of the last two nights without sleep suddenly hit me. My feet warmed a little and I thought of the afternoon visit. The wing was silent except for the occasional roars of laughter from 'B—' and 'C—'. 'B—' would be back after dinner, drunk and dangerous, I thought. I closed my eyes hoping to escape for a while through sleep till dinner-time. God, it's hard. It's very hard.

I rose slowly from the mattress testing every movement. I made it to my feet and placed the mattress against the wall. I spread a blanket on the floor and with another blanket wrapped around my waist and a towel around my head and shoulders I set off once again like a nomad on my journey to nowhere. It was still cold but the morning bite had gone from the air. The snow still lay heavy on the ground outside and the light was unusually dim for midday.

The dinner will be here shortly, I thought, and then it's only a few hours to my visit. The thought of seeing my family was comforting. It was the highlight and only highlight of each long torturous month. Twelve highlights per year! Half an hour of comparative happiness each visit. That's six hours of comparative happiness a year. I did a quick bit of mental arithmetic; that's six hours out of 8,760 per year. Six lousy hours and they harass you and your family for every minute of it, every single minute of it!

I walked on, anger beginning to surge up inside me. 'Bastards,' I said and stopped to gaze out of the open but concrete barred window. I won't have this much longer either, I reminded myself, thinking of how they'd started to block up the windows in the other wings with corrugated iron and timber, blocking out all sunlight and the sky. There wasn't much to see anyway except the birds, the night sky and the clouds. The rest was just a downright depressing eyesore although at present the snow was unusual and it hung on the miles of ugly, gruesome barbed wire and clung to the impersonal, usually depressing, corrugated iron. Everything was either a dreary grey or a brilliant white. At night there would be a bit of colour while the snow lasted, with the thousands of assorted bright lights and beaming spotlights reflecting on the white carpet.

Wouldn't it be a relief and delight to stroll through a lush green field and touch the blades of shining grass and feel the fresh texture of a leaf on a tree or sit on a hill and gaze upon a valley filled with the buzzing life of spring, smelling the fresh clean, healthy scent with nothing but miles of space around me.

Freedom: that was it. Freedom to live again. I turned from the window to continue my relentless pacing, disheartened a little by the thoughts of freedom. I looked at the stinking, dirt-covered walls, the piles of disease-ridden rubbish and decaying waste food that lay scattered in the corners on the damp floor. The mutilated, filthy mattress, torn to shreds by a thousand searches. The tea-stained ceiling, to cut the glare reflecting off the bright light, the scraped and scarred door, and the disease-ridden chamber-pot that lay beside the door. It was getting harder and harder to conjure up the picture of that beautiful lush green field. Every minute my nightmarish surroundings screamed at me. There was no escaping this nightmare unless I gave up! A few — a very few — had already given up. They had put on prison clothes and conformed. Not that they had wished to do this. They just couldn't bear the unrelenting burden of torture, the continued boredom, tension and fear, the deprivation of basic necessities like exercise and fresh air, no association with other human beings except through a shout from behind a closed heavy steel door.

The depression, the beatings, the cold — what is there I said to myself? Look out the window and concentration camp screams at you. Look around you in the tomb that you survive in and you are engulfed in hell, with little black devils in the forms of 'A—', 'B—' and 'C—' ready to pounce on you each minute of each stinking nightmare-ridden day.

I pulled my mattress back to its former position on the floor and sat down. The first clouds of depression fell upon me. I tried to think of my coming visit to cheer myself up. I thought of Pee Wee and I was about to kill 'B—' and 'C—' in another fantasy, when a cheer arose announcing the arrival of the long-awaited dinner. The 'Happy Wagon', as they called the lorry that brought the food from the cook house to the H-Blocks, had arrived. And thank God for that, I thought, forgetting the threatening depression. There was a bit of a buzz in the wing as signs of life suddenly appeared from within the tombs around me. A few of the lads went to the windows and a bit of chatter ensued. The arrival of the dinner did not only mean food. It also meant that the screws would be departing shortly for their two hour dinner break. It meant comparative safety for two short hours and it also meant that you would only have half a day left to battle with. A slight drizzle of rain fell outside. I hoped to God it wouldn't rain heavily for if the snow melted they'd be out with the hoses, hosing the outside of the cells and the yards. That meant we'd get hosed down with the high-powered apparatus. In this weather we'd freeze to death if we or our bedding were saturated. It's murder trying to hide in the corner to escape the powerful jet of freezing water. With no panes of glass in the windows there's nothing to stop it.

A lock shuddered and a door opened.

'Dinner up!' one of the lads shouted in Gaelic.

I abruptly forgot about the high-powered hose and headed towards my little peep-hole. They were moving down the far side of the wing. I'd get my dinner last, I thought. The plastic plates were piled on top of each other on the trolley. The orderlies were handing them into each cell. 'B—' stood breaking off pieces of fish from the plates and was in the process of eating them. I was raging.

'Fenian steaks for dinner,' 'B—' was shouting. He was laughing at his own sick wit.

'I hope they choke on them,' said 'C—', putting his little dig in as usual. The food procession moved on with 'A—' bringing up the rear. They reached the bottom of the wing and turned. I heard the doors on my side of the wing opening and slamming as they drew nearer.

'B—' shouted, 'Mr "A—", there seems to be a fish short.'

A sickening feeling hit me right in the chest, almost crippling me. I was the last man. That stinking bastard 'B—' ate it. I felt like screaming it out the door, but that was what they wanted me to do.

'Ah! Mr "A—",' said 'B—'. 'I seem to have made a mistake. There's not a fish missing at all.'

My heart lifted.

'There's two missing, Mr "A—"!'

I thought Seán was going to go through the door. I knocked on the wall quickly to remind him that he wasn't on his own. I could hear him cursing them up and down. I felt as sick as the fish must have felt when it was hooked. The most eatable part of the dinner would be missing. It was a catastrophe and Seán knew it as well as I did.

Seán's door opened and closed. Then mine opened. I stood there as if nothing had occurred. I took the sparse-looking meal from the orderly as 'A—' drawled, 'We seem to be a few fish short. I shall inform the cook house to send them to us as soon as possible.'

That really meant, 'Too bad you are not getting any.'

I caught a glimpse of 'B—' ceremoniously licking his fingers while wearing that hateful smile of his for the occasion. I turned away from the door not having uttered a single word or given them any hint of my utter disgust and dejection. The door slammed like a cannon-shot behind me. They all had a jolly good laugh on their way back to their little office, orderlies and all.

I sat down and inspected my meagre dinner of one unpeeled cold potato and about thirty or forty equally cold and hard peas. The orderlies began their daily session of drumming out and whistling *The Sash My Father Wore*. 'B—' would see them right with a few cigarettes, crack a few sectarian jokes with them and encourage them to keep up their incessant racket. The orderlies, for their stinking part, crawled right up his sectarian ass and grovelled as only informers and rabble can grovel. They'd sell their own mothers for a cigarette. What they did to us for the same price and an easy time of it, would make their poor mothers sick.

I began to salvage some of the cold dinner, eating as much as I could which was an effort, and throwing the left-overs into the corner with the rest of the filth and rubbish.

The Sash My Father Wore ceased and a few seconds later the cell doors began opening to the shouts of 'Collecting the dishes', which echoed along the wing. I began walking, not bothering to have a sly look out of the peep-hole. They continued on their way, collecting the dishes and moving from one cell to the next. I heard Seán telling his neighbour to tell the O/C that he was going to ask the screw for bog roll (toilet paper).

The thoughts of my afternoon visit were getting the better of my nervous system, the excitement in just the thought was getting the better of my constipated bowels of five days as they began to churn.

The party had reached Seán's door.

'Any chance of a bit of toilet paper, mister?' asked Seán.

'Wipe it with your hand,' snapped 'C—' and slammed the door.

One and all went into hysterics over 'C—'s' sick wit! My cell door opened, the orderly removed the plate in the midst of the hilarious uproar. No mention of my missing fish, just 'B—'s' chirping 'That was a good one Mr "C—",' and then more convulsions of laughter.

'Ah, no doubt Mr "C—", a cracker. Ha, ha, ha, ha!'

The door slammed. 'C—' delighted in humiliating us. There was an excuse for 'B—'. He had the mentality of an idiot. 'A—' revelled in it, and the four orderlies competed with each other to win their stinking favour. I rapped on the wall.

'Seán,' I called, 'I'll rig up a line with a bit of towel thread and swing a few tissues into you, *mo chara*.

'Hold on till the screws go for their dinner,' I added.

'*Maith thú,* Bobby,' he said. I sat down again to engineer the line, tearing long bits of thread from the towel and twining them together. Just about made 'C—'s' day that, I thought, working away at my line.

'Mr "B—", are you on the night-guard tonight?' enquired a screw from the top of the wing.

'Yes, that's right,' 'B—' shouted back from the office.

'Ho! Ho! Good or bad?' I asked myself. He'll be going home now but he'll back at 8.30 tonight for the night-guard. He'll be drunk — and I knew right away what that meant.

'You hear that, Bobby?' shouted Seán.

'I heard it, comrade,' I answered, thinking Seán had reached the same conclusion as myself.

'Trouble tonight!'

I stood up and lifted a small half rotten potato from the rubbish and tied it on to the end of the completed line to weight it. The office door slammed, and the hated keys jingled. They were going and good riddance to them, I said, going to the window and tying several tissues on to the end of my line. I knocked on the wall.

'You there, Seán?'

'I'm here, Bobby,' he said.

'Well, put your hand out and I'll swing these tissues to you,' I said.

I put my arm out the open window and began swinging the weighted line across the five foot gap. It hit Seán's hand a few times before he caught hold of it.

'I've got it, Bobby,' he said.

'*Maith thú*, Seán. Take it to you,' I said.

He pulled the line in and secured the badly needed

tissues and then rapped on the wall in acknowledgement. I answered with a knock on the wall, and retreated into my thoughts again. What else could I think of but my visit — seeing my family again. And I'd get a smoke too. That was something to look forward to. It had been a long while since I'd seen a cigarette and with a bit of luck I'd have some tonight for myself and the boys. That would be an achievement and a morale booster!

My bowels began to churn again. That's it, I thought, and in a way it was a welcome thought after five days of severe constipation, I'm going to have to go to the toilet, which sounded a bit ridiculous, as I lifted some tissues and retreated to the corner of my cell which did not afford a view from the spy hatch in the cell door. Despite the relief from constipation I felt like an animal squatting in the corner of the cell among the rubbish and dirt. But there was nothing else for it. It had to be done, however humiliating and degrading. More so to the lads who were two to a cell. At least I had some privacy!

Who among those so-called humanitarians who had kept their silence on the H-Blocks, who among them could put a name on this type of humilitation and torture, when men are forced by extreme torture into the position that they had to embark upon a dirt strike to highlight the inhumanity poured upon them! How much must we suffer, I thought. An unwashed body, naked and wrecked with muscular pain, squatting in a corner, in a den of disease, amid piles of putrifying rubbish, forced to defecate upon the ground where the excreta would lie and the smell would mingle with the already sickening evil stench of urine and decaying waste food. Let them find a name for that sort of torture, I thought, rising and moving towards the window to seek fresh air, the beatings, the hosing-downs, starvation and deprivation, just let them bloody well put a name on this nightmare of nightmares.

The drizzle had ceased and the snow remained intact. I was not so cold now but a chill remained. There were several sparrows trudging about on the snow searching for food, which brought to mind again the fish that I never got, nor would ever get! I gathered a few crusts of bread from the floor and flung them out the window to the smaller citizens, the sparrows, and stood watching them pecking their little hearts out. Many an hour I passed at this window just watching the birds, I thought. The sparrows and starlings, crows and seagulls were my constant companions, and the little wagtails who stayed to entertain me, fluttering about the yard until the last shadows of day departed. They were my only form of entertainment during the long boring days and they came every day now since I began throwing the crusts of bread out to them. They liked the maggots, I thought, thinking of the sweltering summer months when the cells were like ovens and the stench from the putrifying piles of rubbish and decaying waste food was almost overwhelming. That was when the white, wriggling, crawling maggots made their way out of the rubbish piles in their thousands.

I'll never forget that, I said to myself, reflecting on the morning I woke up and my blankets and mattress were a living mass of white maggots. They were in my hair and beard and crawling upon my naked body. They were repulsive, and dare I say it, frightening at first. But like everything else I had come to terms with them sharing my cell with me. At night I could hear them actually moving about the floor, disturbing little bits of paper, now and again causing a rustling noise as they headed in the direction of my mattress, where they would finally embed themselves and in the warmth harden into an egg-like cocoon before hatching into flies. They would give off a sharp crack whenever I stood on them in my bare feet in the darkness, squashing them. Needless to say their end product was a pest and very annoying, hundreds of fat bloated flies that clung to the ceiling and walls, continually pestering my naked body day and night, hovering around my face as I tried to sleep or awakening me in the mornings when I would catch a glimpse of a black cloud ascending in panic as I stirred. But the maggots had another use, as I quickly discovered. I soon became so used to them that I would gather them up in my hands off the floor and from the rubbish piles in the corners. There would be thousands of them wriggling and sliding about. Having gathered them together between my palms, I would throw the white wriggling mass out of the window, scattering them over the jet-black tarmacadam yard and against the black background their white wriggling little forms were easily spotted. The wagtails came fluttering about in a frenzy, their quick little legs darting them from one maggot to the next, feasting upon what to them must have been a delicacy. Within two or three minutes the yard would be cleared of every single maggot. I suppose it was something to do, to pass the time. Who would believe it if you told them you spent your summer gathering maggots to feed the birds?

I lifted a few crusts of bread from the corner and flung them out the window remembering my little friends again. Winter was a hard time for the birds, with the snow coating the ground and hiding the land.

I went back to my pacing once again as one of the boys shouted *Rang anois* summoning the lads to their doors for an Irish language class.

The teacher was at the far end of the wing. He began to shout out the lessons at the top of his voice from behind his heavy steel door, asking questions, spelling out words and phrases, while the willing pupils scratched and scribbled them upon the dirty mutilated walls. It was a rough and rugged way of teaching but it worked, and everyone endeavoured to speak what they learned all the time until the words and phrases became so common that they were used instinctively. The Irish class continued in the background as I returned to my thoughts. Thinking of how they would be getting ready in the house now to come up on the afternoon visit, if they weren't on their way already. They were probably as excited as I was, wishing the time away.

It would be a long hard day for them, waiting and queuing, being herded about like cattle from one gate to the next. From one degrading search to another. Enduring the insults and despising, dirty glances from the screws before they finally reached the visit-box. Then they would have to go though it all again to get out.

A screw began jeering and shouting from the top of the wing trying to disrupt the on-going Gaelic class but the lads continued, disregarding him. It happened all the time. The screws, achieving nothing, soon got fed up and departed. I sat down upon the mattress again, my body still sore, the bruises colouring more as each hour passed by. I was very tired, becoming easily exhausted, not having had exercise or fresh air for so long, and I was bored stiff. The thought of my afternoon visit left me barely able to think. But there is always someone worse off than yourself, I told my-self, remembering only too well my dead comrades and their families.

'At least I can see you once a month,' my mother would say. 'Better where you are than Milltown Cemetery.'*

But then there were times when Milltown would have been the preferable alternative when things became so unbearable that you just couldn't care less whether you lived or died just as long as you could escape the hellish nightmare. Aren't we dying any-way, I thought. Aren't our bodies degenerating to a standstill? I am a living corpse now. What will I be like in six months' time? Will I even be alive after another year? I used to worry about that, churning it around in

* Bobby was eventually buried in Milltown Cemetery.

my mind for hours on end. But no more! Because that is the only thing left that they can do to me: kill me. I have known this for sometime and God knows that it isn't for the want of trying that they haven't achieved that on some one of us yet! But I am determined that I shall never give up. They can do what they will with me but I will never bow to them or allow them to criminalise me.

I find it startling to hear myself say that I am pre-pared to die first rather than succumb to their oppress-ive torture and I know that I am not on my own, that many of my comrades hold the same. And I thought of my dead comrades again. My friends who had stood beside me one day and were dead the next. Boys and girls just like myself, born and raised in the nationalist ghettos of Belfast to be murdered by foreign soldiers and lecky sectarian thugs. How many have been murdered at their hands throughout the occupied Six Counties. Too many! One boy or girl was one too many! How many more Irish people would die? How many more lives would be lost before the British had decided they had murdered enough and were forced to get out of Ireland forever? Inside and outside of gaol it was all the same — oppression bearing down upon you from every direction. Every street corner displaying an armed British soldier, every street having endured its share of suffering and grief at their hands.

I was proud to be resisting, to be fighting back. They couldn't defeat us outside; they are torturing us unmercifully inside their hell-holes and have failed to defeat us again. I was frightened but I knew I would never give up. I would face the imperial might of their entire torturous arsenal rather then succumb. I tugged at my blankets to wrap them round me and rolled over hoping to doze for a while. The screws would not be back until after two o'clock. 'B—' would be back at 8.30 pm tonight and I wondered who would be his replacement meantime. I'll find out soon enough, I thought, closing my eyes and my mind to my surroundings.

'Slop out on the air! Slop out on the air!'
I awoke with a jump.
'Slop out on the air!'
The tin bucket clammered and rattled and a cold chill swept through my body leaving an empty hollow sensation in the pit of my stomach. I rose quickly but wearily, dreading the thought of a cramp. I was okay, although for several seconds my eyes fought to clear the blackness of a light head and threatening blackout.

I defeated it and sprang to my peep-hole at the door. The door next to Pee Wee's cell opened. 'A—', 'B—' and, 'C—'s' replacement, 'D—', stood in a semi-circle around the entrance, the four grovelling orderlies flanking them, one clutching a squeegee (a pole with a rubber fitting used to push pools of water down drains). John O'Brien stepped into the doorway, his blanket hanging around him, and emptied his chamber-pot of urine on to the ground in the wing, then stepped back into the cell. The orderly with the squeegee needed no signal. He stepped forward and brushed the pool of urine back into the cell again, all around John O'Brien's mattress. Most of the lads were lashing the contents of their pos under the doors using the empty po to push the urine that remained out into the wing. The bottom of my door was too tight. There was a large gap at the top and side, but too awkward for this type of operation. I would have to take the hard way out and heave it into the wing as John O'Brien had done when the door opened. It had to be done. If they got a po of urine in your cell it would end up over you and your bedding. There is more than one way to skin a cat or, in our case, more than one way to try to break a Prisoner-of-War, and this was a well-worn one. They were switching cells, going from one side of the wing to the other. It didn't matter whose door they opened, it was just another harassment exercise, a build-up to more torture. I grabbed the po and stood poised for action! Better if I had had a cell mate, I thought, wishing for moral support. But Seán was on his own as well, and so was poor Pee Wee this morning. They were going to get someone else, I could sense that this was the whole object of the slop out, and we all knew that only too well.

My lock rattled, alerting me. I stood poised and ready, po in hand, hoping for the best. The door opened. I didn't even glance at them. I lowered the po towards the ground, jettisoning the contents in the middle of the manoeuvre, hoping none would splash around their stinking, shining boots. I stepped back, lifting my head, expecting a blow that never came. I glanced at their faces. 'C—' and 'D—' were steaming drunk. 'A—' was grinning as usual. The orderly appeared and began to brush the reeking mess back into my cell saturating the sides and bottom of my mattress before he decided to retreat. The door slammed. I lifted my mattress and began squeezing the urine out of the filthy foam on to the floor. I then started to scrape and push the pool towards the bottom of the door. It was a long slow process. The door was tight and narrow. The urine trickled out slowly. In the wing the slop out continued. The bucket rattled, spelling out danger. The occasional splash announced another emptied po. The tension was almost sickening.

Then it happened. A sudden eruption of noise, shouts, yells and venom-filled screams. The bucket clammered on to the ground and a barrage of dull thuds carried along the wing. What sounded like someone's head colliding with the steel pipes came ringing through the cells. I dropped my po and put my eye to the peep-hole, hearing a voice scream, 'Give them more!' The ruckus continued until I heard 'A—' shout, 'That's enough!' Several screws came tearing down the wing from the opposite direction, their heavy boots squelching and splashing in the pools of reeking urine that lay on the corridor floor.

'Get a van for the punishment cells,' screamed 'D—' in his hateful, ignorant voice. There were more thuds and banging, then footsteps and evil laughter, followed by the gradual build-up of running feet, bumping and what sounded like the swish of water. Four black uniforms darted past my area of vision dragging a naked body by the feet, his back scraping and scratching the ground and his head bumping off the concrete. It passed so quickly that I was unable to recognise who it was. But there had been blood on his face and body whoever he was.

For several seconds nothing stirred. A sinister, expectant silence resumed. The pools of urine rippled and waved, then settled into a calm pool just as the same noises built up again; the speedy build-up of feet gaining speed, the thuds, bangs and swish, as another mass of black figures soared past my line of vision dragging another blood-stained body by the feet. The swish died away and the squeaks of the naked body burning as it reached and contacted the dry, shiny surface at the end of the wing, faded. The sinister silence resumed its ugly role. Tension hung like a guillotine. No one dared to breathe aloud, fearing it would fall upon them. It was soul-destroying and seemingly endless. A scream came shrieking and hurtling down the wing.

'Tiocfaidh ár lá!' bounced and rebounded in frightening echoes off the walls, shattering the silence like the impact of a brick crashing through a window, raising hearts, bitterness and hate rivetted to every single syllable. 'Our day will come!' That's what it meant and our day would come, I told myself, and God help you, 'A—', 'C—' and 'D—' and you too, 'B—' and every stinking last one of you, because you are all the same — torture-mongers.

'Tiocfaidh ár lá!' I screamed out the door. One of

the boys down the wing began to sing. *A Nation Once Again* resounded and echoed from behind every door and everyone joined in to break that ungodly silence, lifting our spirits and bolstering our shaken morale. The stench from the reeking urine streamed in through the door flooding my eyes with tears and catching the back of my throat. The orderlies attempted a rendering of *The Sash*, but were drowned out with an explosion of noise as the now empty pos rattled and battered the scarred doors in defiance and anger.

'*Tiocfaidh ár lá!* All right!' I said, 'and the sooner the better.'

I went back to my task of getting rid of the small remaining pool of urine at my feet, pushing it out under the door. The noise began to die away as the last drops of urine disappeared in a trickle out the door. I threw the po into the corner upon the rubbish and sat down on my mattress, my feet avoiding the damp area, my mind in a turmoil, exhausted and strained, begging relief and comfort that was never granted.

The noise died completely. Seán rapped on the wall, concerned as ever.

'All right, Bobby?' he called.

'I'm all right, Seán. What about yourself?'

'They didn't even come to my cell,' he replied.

'Who was dragged out?' I asked.

'I don't know,' he said, adding that he had sent down the line to find out.

'But I think that "C—" and "D—" did all the beating,' he said.

'They probably did,' I offered in agreement.

'Hey Seán!' one of the lads shouted up the line, 'it was Liam Clarke and Seán Hughes. "C—" and "D—" did most of the beating. The orderly with the squeegee beat the two lads stupid with the pole. No reason, Seán. Same as usual. They pounced on them when they were turning back into the cell.'

I left Seán to discuss with the lads at the windows what had happened and began walking the floor once again, keeping in mind that I could be called for my visit at any minute. The beating up of the two lads — and Pee Wee O'Donnell earlier — had temporarily dampened my enthusiasm. I couldn't help but think of them lying there now on the boards, in the punishment block, where they probably got another brutal beating at the hands of the sadistic screws who appropriately managed that torture centre within a torture centre.

I knew only too well what it was like in there. It was dreaded by one and all. The punishment block stood for torture, brutality and inhumanity. Even the screws knew it but would not say. I spent three days there a few months ago — three of the longest and most unbearable days of my entire life. The screws removed me from my cell naked and I was conveyed to the punishment block in a blacked-out van. As I stepped out of the van on arrival there they grabbed me from all sides and began punching and kicking me to the ground. Not one single word had been spoken, not even so much as a threat. I was a Republican blanketman and that was all the go-ahead that was needed. I barely realised what had occurred or what was happening as they dragged me by the hair across a stretch of hard core rubble to the gate of the punishment block. One of them rang the bell to summon the screw inside to come out and open the gate to admit them. I lay at their feet, dazed, shocked and panting for breath. My heart was pounding and my body felt like it was on fire, torn to ribbons by the rough concrete that had cut and hacked at my naked skin. My face was warm and wet from the blood spurting from a gash on my head. I lay stock still, playing 'possum, hoping they'd be content thinking that I was unconscious. My cheek rested upon the cold hard black surface but my body was unaware of the biting cold. I mumbled a 'Hail Mary' to myself and a hurried 'Act of Contrition' as I heard the approaching jingle of keys. Several gloved hands gripped and tightened around my arms and feet raising my body off the ground and swinging me backwards in the one movement. The full weight of my body recoiled forward again, smashing my head against the corrugated iron covering around the gate. The sky seemed to fall upon me as they dropped me to the ground. The second impact sent a mass of tiny white stars exploding in front of my eyes like a fireworks display that suddenly became extinguished by a cloud of inky blackness. I regained consciousness lying on the floor of one of the cells in the punishment block.

I opened my eyes. My head was reeling. The bright light in the ceiling spiralled downwards and blinded me. The pain in my head was enormous and sickening. My whole body was seized by crippling pains and aches. I lay transfixed to the ground, afraid to move, the taste of blood on my swollen lips, fighting to work out where I was and what had happened. The concrete floor was intensely cold and I knew I would have to get off it or pay the consequences of perhaps pneumonia later. I rose slowly to my knees first. The walls came hurtling towards me. I fell. After an eternity I tried again though spasms of pain almost rendered my body useless. I made it to my knees. My skin was burning as the raw flesh from the mass of cuts and scrapes clung to the cold floor. I got up. I made it to my feet. I almost fell again but with the aid of the wall I staggered to the concrete block that served as a stool and slumped upon it. I felt as if I were dying. I was so distracted by pain and shock that I didn't know what to do. I simply couldn't think. The slightest movement of my body sent me shivering and gasping in agony. I was on the point of screaming out when the cell door opened revealing a white-coated figure of an orderly who stepped into the cell. The glorified screw with the white coat began to examine me, fiddling about my body, poking and probing, imitating the antics of a doctor, trying to impress the audience of screws who stood around the entrance of the cell.

Having made his observations, or whatever he had done, he arrogantly informed me that to see the doctor and receive treatment I would firstly have to bathe. I glared at him in disbelief. He repeated what he had said only in a sterner threatening voice. He knew what he was doing. He knew I was hurt and in need of immediate attention, but he was putting me under duress, holding me to ransom. No bath — no treatment. Besides, I was so sore I could barely move let alone bathe and I hadn't any intention of breaking my protest. Hurt or dying I was not going to concede to him or anyone else. I knew what was coming. His ultimatum changed to a command.

'Drop dead!' I said angrily. The hovering press-gang without so much as 'Where are you hurt?' and without any ceremony lifted me as a man would lift a bundle of rags and carried me to the already-full bath, dropping me into the water like a bar of soap. The shock of the ice-cold water engulfing my tattered body almost stopped my breath.

Every part of me stung unmercifully as the heavily disinfected water attacked my naked raw flesh. I made an immediate and brave attempt to rise out of the freezing, stinging water but the screws held me down while one of them began to scrub my already tattered back with a heavy scrubbing brush. I shrivelled with the pain and struggled for release but the more I fought the more they strengthened their iron grip. The tears came flooding to my eyes. I would have screamed had I been able to catch my breath. They continued to scrub every part of my tortured body, pouring buckets of ice cold water and soapy liquid over me. I vaguely remember being lifted out of the cold water — the sadistic screw had grabbed my testicles and scrubbed my private parts. That was the last thing I remembered. I collapsed.

I was taken to the prison hospital wrapped in a large

fawn blanket where the doctor examined me. I remained there for two hours and patched up like a mummy, sporting a black eye and seven stitches in my head, I was returned to my punishment cell. I sat there wrapped in a solitary filthy blanket that reeked of urine and stale smoke. I had regained my composure although I was a little disorientated and still trying to piece together my awful ordeal. But that soon became overshadowed by the thoughts of what was to come. No one could do anything for me. I could not tell a soul as I was isolated, alone and vulnerable. I was simply at their mercy and I had already discovered and learned that they did not know the meaning of the word. Perhaps worst of all I was freezing cold, unable to walk and exercise to warm myself and I was feeling sorry for myself. The screws came back later in the day and once again dragged me out of the cell to appear naked before a Prison Governor to be tried in the normal farcical court. I stood naked before them, humiliated and embarrassed, my head bursting with the pain from my earlier beating. I was charged with 'disobeying an order' — that is refusing to co-operate with the screw who was endeavouring to probe and search my anal passage. In other words, I refused point-blank to allow this. But I was charged because it took three or four of them to hold me down to do it. The screw in question had been the white-coated one. It would have made little difference to me had he been a brain surgeon, as the motive was purely to degrade and humiliate me, which was all part of the general torture to break our resistance. I was found guilty — not that I expected anything else — and sentenced to three days to be spent in the punishment cells, to be fed on what was politely termed a 'number one diet', a starvation diet. I also lost one month's remission, the equivalent of a two month prison sentence! To wrap things up nicely, I was charged with assaulting the four screws who had almost murdered me that morning and, to rub it in, I was also charged with causing self-inflicted wounds to myself and informed in a roundabout way that if I dared to make a formal complaint I would also be charged with making false allegations against prison officers. How can you win, I thought, and felt like vomiting as they dragged me back to my cell again, being remanded to appear before the Board of Visitors. I would be here three days, then back again at the end of the month for another fifteen days. The B.O.V.s would ensure that.

The cell was freezing cold, bare and lonely. I'd been here once before therefore I knew just how lonely and unbearable it would get. A board on the concrete floor served as my bed, a concrete slab as a table and a concrete block as a stool. A bible, po and water container were the only other visible items. I remained there for the three days, being beaten up twice more but not as severely as the initial hiding I received. When the filth in the po needed to be emptied they attempted to hold me to ransom.

'Put on prison clothes to empty it,' they said.

I refused. So it spilled over on to the cell floor and lay there. I plodded through it regardless. I had to get warm. My body was continuously numb. For the first two days I was barely able to walk at all and I was growing weaker as the starvation diet took its toll. My daily food consisted of two slices of bread, dry and stale, and a mug of black luke-warm tea for breakfast. Then for dinner I had a small bowl of watery soup. My evening tea was the same as breakfast. On the third day I collapsed once again and lay upon the cold concrete floor regaining consciousness sometime later of my own accord.

When I returned to H-Block even the screws stared in shock at my death-like appearance. I was physically wrecked and mentally exhausted. The starvation, beatings, forcible bathing, the boredom and cold remained in my mind, scarring me deeply with hatred, bitterness and thoughts of revenge. Two weeks later I endured another fifteen days there. It was the same nightmare only multiplied by five. I lived like an insane animal, eating with my hands. Every other three days they starved me and once again I plodded through the dirt and filth, exercising to keep warm, taking the beatings, praying to myself, crying in my sleep, always fighting the urge to give in to them, to surrender.

But I survived. I beat them again. The torturous dungeons and the sadists who manned them had destroyed my body but had failed to break my spirit. It was three weeks later before I recovered from my torturous ordeal. My mind will never recover from it. God only knows how many of us have been subjected to that nightmare. Poor Pee Wee and the other two lads will be going through it all now. How many more will be subjected to it and how long can it go on before someone is beaten to death, I wondered. 'Where is it all going to end?' I asked myself, sitting down upon my mattress again.

The afternoon was growing older and the first tinges of worry began to cross my mind. Where was my visit? I sat listening and willing the 'phone at the top of the wing to ring to inform 'A—' that my visitors had arrived. I began stripping pieces of thread from one of my flimsy blankets and started to plait them together to pass the time, making a long line that hopefully would come in handy later. A skiff of snow fell in through the open window as another heavy fall threatened to follow once more. The afternoon light was beginning to fade, growing dimmer with each passing minute. The cawing of the crows making their way home from the nearby fields came plainly on the slight evening breeze. I rose and stood at the window watching the crows fade into the distance and the thousands of different coloured lights illuminating their designated vicinity one by one, as they were switched on. The entire area before my eyes was soon a mass of brilliant lights, causing the snow-coated wire to sparkle and glitter. The winter light of day died and darkness took over. It was getting very late, I thought, hiding the plaited line in a hole in my mattress and feeling the ever-increasing panic setting in more and more. I was wondering and speculating as to what could have happened to my visit. It must be at least 4.30 pm, I thought. What has happened? The telephone rang. I stiffened my muscles hoping to hear the long-awaited words. 'A—' was summoned by the screw at the top of the wing. That's it, I thought excitedly and sat down impatiently awaiting developments. The minutes dragged by and still no indication to confirm that my visit had arrived. Five minutes! Now ten minutes! Then the rattle of keys and approaching footsteps. The warning rattle of the lock and the door opened. 'C—' and 'D—' stood there.

'Visit, tramp,' 'C—' rasped at me, hatred hanging to every syllable. If 'C—' had his way I would be put up against the nearest wall to be shot. I rose from the mattress pulling the blankets off me, letting them drop to the ground and wrapping a towel around me. I stepped out of the cell door into the urine-covered corridor of the wing.

It was warmer in the corridor than it was in the cells. I noticed that immediately. I trod on through the river of urine until I reached the end cell where the prison garb was stored. Going on a visit was the only time that we donned the prison uniform. I glanced around me and grabbed the nearest set of clothing. I was just about to put on the shirt when 'D—' said, 'Right! Drop your towel and stand over by that mirror,' pointing to a large mirror which lay on the floor. I did as he said. He then told me to bend over and touch my toes. I refused. 'A—' was called and he entered the cell. All three of them proceeded to grab me and forcibly bend me over. 'A—' and 'D—' held me while 'C—' inspected my anus. After several seconds they released their grip and I straightened myself up and began to dress.

'Bastards,' I said to myself. They didn't even ask me

to open my mouth. They were not interested in searching me but in humiliating me!

I left the cell, dressed and disgusted, storing in the back of my mind the fact that they didn't search my mouth and reminding myself that the worst had yet to come! They locked me between the steel grills at the top of the wing. I was a sorrowful-looking sight: dirty face, shaggy hair and beard, with the prison uniform that was several sizes too large hanging on me. I didn't give a damn. But the sooner I got it off me the better and to hell with my appearance! I was being tortured not manicured. A screw came and opened the gate of the grill whereupon another screw awaited to escort me to my visit. He led me out and into a blacked-out transit van that sat outside the door of the yard, engine running and the exhaust smoke belching out underneath the back of it into the darkness. I shivered as I sat down upon the hard bench-like seat. I had been hoping that some of the lads from the other wings or Blocks might have been in the van going on a visit also but it was empty and dark. My escorting screw climbed into the back of the van and closed the door over throwing the confines into total darkness.

'Right!' he shouted to the van driver who immediately drove off. We passed out through the front gate of the H-Blocks — the front gate of Hades, I thought to myself. The screw cursed the loose rattling door and held it to stop it flying open. He tried to make conversation with me.

'How long have you been on the blanket now?' he enquired, and added immediately, 'Don't you think you'd be as well packing it in?'

'No, I don't,' I answered him dryly.

'Yous aren't getting nowhere,' he said matter-of-factly.

'No one ever does until they reach what they set out for,' I said sharply.

'You must be mad,' he said. 'I wouldn't do what you are doing if I were in your position.'

'I'm quite sure you wouldn't,' I said. 'Maybe that's because you're a screw and I'm a Political Prisoner.' He didn't like that last remark, I thought, as he became very quiet in the darkness. 'I'm sure his face is red,' I said to myself.

'Besides,' I said, putting the boot right in, 'at the end of the day you will be entitled to feel more let down than anyone.'

'How's that?' he muttered.

'Well,' I added, 'when the British government, through the stroke of a political pen grant political status to us again or, better still, declare their intention to withdraw, which they will do all right when necessity forces them to, it's going to make a proper ass out of you. What are you going to do then?'

'That won't ever happen,' he said nervously.

'It will happen all right,' I said. 'And better still they've done it before in places like Cyprus, Aden and Palestine. Yes, they will most certainly do it again,' I added just for good measure as the van came to an abrupt halt. He opened the door and stepped out, beckoning me to follow him. He wasn't so chirpy now, I noticed. It frightened the best of them. None of

71

them relished the thought of being left high and dry, especially with the atrocities that they had committed, and still were committing, to be answered for. I passed by the search boxes that were doing a brisk trade on those returning from their visits. They were all remand prisoners and ordinary prisoners. The special search hut for blanket-men was set apart from all the other huts, looking sinister and evil. Patches of snow were clinging to the sides of its wooden structure, giving it a lonely, desolate appearance but it was in operation all right. A heavy dull thud and a shout coming from its interior soon testified to that.

I entered the visiting building and stood there in the bright light while the screw went to find out what visiting box I was to be brought to. Dozens of screws eyed me up and down as they passed me by, making the occasional snide remark and jibe at me. I ignored them. The bustle around me seemed unreal. I was unused to such a change in atmosphere. It was not the murderous tension-filled atmosphere that surrounded and hung over me every day in the H-Block. There were plenty of nasty screws here all right, but they were concerned with other business which, thank God, wasn't me for a change!

The screw came back and led me to a large visiting room.

'Box 7,' he said.

'Jesus,' I thought, 'Box 7 is one of the end boxes where most of the prowling screws congregated.' The screw opened the visiting room door and I walked into a large room. It was like walking into a play. The buzz of whispered conversation struck me first, then the clouds of smoke, the colourful clothing worn by the huddled little groups of visitors who hung over the tables in the open boxes whispering and muttering, the black mass of screws pacing up and down the floor hanging over their shoulders cracking jokes amongst themselves and filling the air with their loud-mouthed laughter. I glanced at the numbering of the boxes, 12, 11, 10, 9, and made my way towards Box 7. Friendly, sympathetic faces smiled encouragement at me from the open boxes. Old women, wives, daughters, sisters and brothers, the children and fathers of my comrades. I smiled back as best I could, feeling more than sorrow and sympathy towards them.

'God bless you, son,' some old woman shouted at me. 'Keep your chin up,' she added.

I felt like crying.

'Move along,' one of the screws snarled at me. In a daze I scanned the boxes as I passed them by. My comrades and their families were smiling and calling to me. I turned into Box 7 and not thinking sat down on the wrong side of the box. The prowling screws nearby nearly ate me.

'Get off that chair and get around to this side of the table,' they snapped, seemingly competing with each other to see who could be the most dominant and nastiest.

I changed sides.

'Bastards,' I said to myself.

'How are you, son?' called some old fella with a Derry accent as he passed by my box.

. 'I'm surviving,' I said, which was just about right and no more!

'Good for you, son and God take care of every one of you,' called another passer-by, a middle-aged woman with what sounded like a Tyrone accent. Some distance to travel, I thought, for a half hour visit.

The screws continued to prowl up and down, ever vigilant and listening to every word that was being spoken. Three more plus my escort stood by the side of my box talking. Three or four people came around the partition directly beside my box. Then my mother appeared, my father and sister following directly behind her. I stood up to greet them as they approached the visiting box. I saw my mother taking a quick glance around her a split second before she started to hug me, then I felt her hand touch the side of the baggy coat that I was wearing. The congregation of screws were partially covered by the approach of my father and sister. Those prowling past the boxes had their backs turned. It was a quick move. I knew what it was and I knew that it was now in my left-hand pocket. My sister had reached me and threw her arms around me while my father shook my hand at the same time. My eyes were scanning the faces of the screws for a tell-tale sign of discovery. There were none but my heart stopped as they moved towards the box. My mother sat down and I sat down beside her. My father and sister went around to the other side of the plain wooden table, which served as the division between prisoner and visitor.

'Right!' shouted a screw.

I nearly fell off the chair, discovery screaming at me from every side.

'You'll have to move away from the prisoner to the other side of the table,' the screw said to my mother.

My heart was pounding and a sickish feeling gripped my chest. I thought for several terrible seconds that I had been caught. That just about would have made my day.

'Prisoner?' my mother said exasperated. 'That's my son. Surely I can sit beside my son?'

'No, I'm afraid you can't,' he said.

'That's right you can't. Prison Rules,' another one chipped in.

I was too busy regaining my composure from the awful fright to argue. My mother, fearing the loss of the visit, somewhat hesitantly moved her chair around to the other side of the table beside my sister and father.

The screws having adamantly stood there to see their word decreed now moved off, retreating a bare three feet from my visiting box, where they stood in a group talking in hushed voices and staring at us all the while. I turned around in my chair turning my back to them and began talking to my family.

'How are you, son?' my mother asked.

'I'm not too bad, Ma,' I answered, seeing the anguish in her face as she examined my terrible appearance.

'Your beard has got a lot longer since I last saw you,' my father said jokingly and my sister began asking me was it cold in the cells. My father took out a packet of cigarettes and gave me one. I took a light from the solitary match that they were allowed to bring with them. My mother held my other hand in her's. I heard the shuffle of feet behind me. I was in no doubt that the warders were watching my every move and weighing every word that was spoken.

'How are you all?' I asked, adding that I thought the three of them looked grand. The cigarette was making my head light but I had dreamed of this cigarette too bloody often to discard it.

'How is everyone else keeping?' I asked, and listened eagerly to the answers. All three competed with each other to get talking. There was so much to be told and so many questions I had to have answered. It was one excited babble of conversation. We ignored our unwanted listeners and reduced our voices to barely audible whispers when something arose that we did not want them to hear. I would have preferred them to hear nothing but what could be done? My father and mother continually glanced towards them but I knew that that would not move them a single inch. My sister was telling me bits and pieces of news. I was trying to lodge them in my mind to tell the lads later while at the same time struggling to remember other things I wished to ask them. My mother whispered to me to be careful with the small parcel in my pocket. She said that there was a little bit of tobacco squashed as small as possible, cigarette papers and a wee note from my sister, Bernadette. My mind was in turmoil, collecting news, asking this and asking that.

Such and such was dead or dying, everyone seemed to be getting married, soldiers wrecked the house again and such and such's young son was charged. There were a lot of strikes brewing here and England was plagued with them. It was in the papers about the 'flu epidemic, the forcible baths and haircutting in the H-Blocks. There had been a Christmas tree on the Falls Road beside Dunville Park, with all the blanket-men's names on it.

I was storing every scrap of information in my mind and all the while thinking of the powder keg in my left-hand pocket. I gave them a quick run-down on things in the Blocks, telling them to drop into the H-Block Information Bureau on the Falls Road and tell them there what I had told them about Pee Wee O'Donnell, Liam Clarke and Seán Hughes and what had occurred during this morning's wing shift. My beard was hiding the marks on my face which I had received that morning but my mother and sister were searching my hands and face for the tell-tale traces of a beating and continually asking me was I sure that I was all right. I lit another cigarette from the one I was about to extinguish, feeling a lot more up to it now. The other visiting boxes were emptying rapidly. I could hear the people moving towards the exit door behind me. I did not look around. I'd seen it all before and didn't wish to see those sorrowful, pitiful faces again. My sister was telling me how her young son was doing. My mother followed that up with what was in last week's *Republican News* and my father added to it.

I gave them a few messages that I had for some of

the lads' families that they could pass on to them. I sat listening intently to how the parade went. My father interjected again to tell me of the growing interest and concern that was gathering in America, France and other European countries over what was going on in the H-Block. Our conversation continued and I lit another cigarette. Twelve minutes left I noted, keeping an eye on my father's watch.

'Good luck to you boys and God bless every one of you,' a departing visitor shouted aloud to one and all. I became conscious of the fact that my unwashed body must be smelling but I ignored it. As ever no comment was forthcoming from my people. My sister was now telling me how things were in the district and who had been around in my mother's house enquiring about me and how her husband was keeping. My mother began to tell me about a recent riot in the district when the screw interrupted her.

'Right, that's it. Time up,' he barked over my shoulder, handing the visiting permit to my mother, emphasising that he wished her, my father and sister to depart.

'There is still eight minutes of my half-hour left,' I said coldly to him.

'Too bad. See the Governor,' was his aggravating reply.

My mother and sister looked towards me anxiously.

'It doesn't matter, son. Sure it's only a couple of minutes,' my mother said, worried that I would reap the repercussions of an argument when they got me outside the visiting area. I rose from the chair knowing that the visit would be over no matter what I said. I was disgusted and angry but I didn't wish to leave my family worrying. There was more than enough to worry over as it was. My mother and sister began hugging and kissing me goodbye, tears rolling down their cheeks having suddenly appeared from nowhere.

I was shattered.

The screws were harassing me from behind.

'Come along, come along. Right. That's enough! Come along!'

'I'll see you next month,' I said to my mother and sister, my father stealing a quick handshake just before the screws literally bundled me towards the exit door for prisoners. I caught a glimpse of the remaining little huddled groups whispering amongst each other around the little tables. In some boxes a screw sat right beside the visitor. These were the notorious 'appeal visits'. One word out of place not pertaining to the appeal case and the watchdog screws sprang upon you and terminated the visit. I caught a final glimpse of my family as they waved goodbye before the screw almost slammed the door in my face.

'Right you!' he roared. 'Wait there!'

He was not my original escort, who had apparently disappeared, but it looked like I was stuck with this bastard who had now gone off to check me out of the visit. I stood there shaking a little, feeling disorientated and somewhat sick, being unused to being out of my small stinking concrete tomb-like cell. The sight of other people with smiles to offer, friendly, sympathetic faces, colourful expressions and clothes, the comfort of just simply seeing my family again was just too much for my physically wrecked body and tortured mind to cope with or adapt to.

There was a bustle of activity going on around me. Screws all over the place.

Jesus, Mary and Holy Saint Joseph! The wee parcel! I worked my hand in panic to the other side of my coat. It was still there. I could feel it. I glanced around and when it looked good put my hand into my pocket and took it out. A screw passed me, eyeing me up and down. I held the wee parcel like a bomb. It was concealed in my fist. I was praying that the screw who was escorting me wouldn't come back now.

All clear. I made my move. Like a flash it was up and out of my hand into my mouth. It was fairly small and wrapped in 'stretch and seal plastic'. I gazed at the window in front of me looking at my reflection. My beard hid any tell-tale bulge. I would just have to sweat it out now. Other screws came walking past me, their searching, probing eyes glaring at me as if I were something out of the ordinary. But then I was, I thought, staring at my reflection in the window again: my uncombed hair ruffled and shaggy and my long beard untamed and wild like a bramble bush, and from somewhere in between, ghostly white and dare I say it somewhat frighteningly, appeared my own face, rugged and aged before its time. My cheeks and eyes were sunken and withdrawn into my face creating a hollow from where my glassy, piercing eyes peered back at me, and unseen and covered by the prison garb, stood my dilapidated, physically-wrecked body.

'Right you, move along,' came that growling bark again, interrupting my thoughts and self-scrutiny, setting me in motion towards the search huts that stood outside. I passed by the first hut where the ordinary prisoners were frisked, searched, and then the second hut where the remand prisoners were dealt with in a similar fashion. The third hut, which I knew only too well, sitting apart from everything else and looking drab, desolate and sinister, was the 'special hut' where only *we* were taken — the blanket-men, the Republican Prisoners-of-War. My escorting screw as ever behind, barked another command, 'Right you, in there!'

I could hardly swallow my spittle with the parcel in my mouth. I detected the eagerness in his voice. He could hardly wait to get me inside. He almost threw me in through the door. The inside of the search hut was as drab as the outside. Several screws stood warming their hands over an oil-fuelled fire. It was cold outside. A coating of snow still lay upon the ground. Panic was rising in me as each of them glared at me, and — as was only to be expected — at my face. I was waiting on the fatal words — 'What's that in your mouth?' But they never came. I stood there for an eternity, my eyes scanning the room. The inside was a lot warmer than the stinking, freezing tomb I was returning to. A few chairs were scattered about the room, a plastic basin filled with a blue-coloured disinfectant sat upon the oil fire where a stack of paper towels lay adjacent to it and upon the floor and looking out-of-place was a large mirror secured to a wooden handle. The screws began to mill around me, batons dangling at their hips. For some stupid reason I thought of a dental surgery! I don't know why, as any dentist that I have ever encountered was considerate.

'Right tramp,' snapped a harsh voice. 'Strip!'

I stripped, standing naked before them. They stood around, glaring at my naked body. I was embarrassed and humiliated, but I couldn't grasp the full significance of it. The humiliation was secondary to my parched throat, the potential bomb in my mouth and the thoughts churning around in my mind of what lay ahead of me. More so if I had to spit out contraband. Jesus! I thought, what they had to do to us to discover and catch the odd love letter from one of the lads' sweethearts, the worrying note from a distracted mother or the lousy meagre little parcel of tobacco! It is just pure torture and harassment.

'Turn around,' growled another bully-boy screw. I turned, making a full circle. Panic gripped me as they scrutinised my body. (I was waiting on the fatal command every second: 'Open your mouth.')

'Turn around again,' snapped the screw who had escorted me.

That's it, I thought, they are really rubbing this humiliation bit in! If I had been able to speak I would have told them that they had humilitated me enough and any more humiliating to be done *they* could do it.

They had forced me to degrade myself enough already. I stood there silent and still. He threatened me and yelled his command once more. I ignored it. I thought the roof had fallen upon them. They were momentarily dumbstruck, so startled that they just stood staring at me in utter disbelief that I had disobeyed their word. Their faces were flushed and perplexed, anger was building up inside them. Here it comes, I told myself, here it bloody well comes!

'Get up against that wall and spread-eagle,' one of them finally mumbled, breaking the seemingly eternal silence. I remained unintimidated but not unperturbed. I was shaking and it wasn't from the cold! I was scared stiff, frightened to the verge of panic. I thought I was about to vomit out the parcel on the floor.

They grabbed my arms and threw me up against the wooden wall. The impact made a dull thud. They held me in spread-eagle fashion. Someone punched me in the ribs and my feet were kicked to part my legs. A terrible pain tore through my outstretched arms and my already aching, bruised body hurt all the more. They continued to hack at my ankles with their heavy issue boots, constantly screaming and shouting, cursing and threatening me.

I felt the cold chamfered edges of the large mirror being pushed between my legs. They were scrutinising my anus using the mirror to afford them a view from every angle. A foreign hand probed and poked at my anus and, unsatisfied, they kicked the back of my knees forcing me down into a squatting position where they again used the mirror and, to finish off, they rained more kicks and blows on my naked, burning body for good measure. I fell to the floor, which was wet and dirty from the melted snow carried into the hut on their boots. I rose immediately, half conscious of the pains as they streaked through my body. I made a desperate attempt to swallow my spittle and not only did I almost choke on the parcel but I almost spat it out on the floor. My face was contorted and red as I fought to hold back a cough. I grabbed the clothing I had been wearing and dressed as quickly as I could, racing to get finished before they finished washing their sadistic hands in the basin of disinfectant.

'Maybe that will help you find your tongue!' rasped one of them, drying his hands with a paper towel. Jesus! I thought, the very mention of anywhere in that vicinity made me panic! I raced to dress. A hand from behind me lifted my hair to see if I had anything hidden behind my ears. I panicked and almost made a move to switch the wee parcel from my mouth to a pocket which they wouldn't search again. But the searching hand withdrew to a vacant space that had just appeared around the disinfectant basin.

Clothes half hanging off me, and realising just how sore I was, I struggled towards the door, my growling companion of a screw falling in behind me. I stepped through the door waiting on — 'Where are you going to? We're not finished,' but again nothing happened.

My throat was burning. The fresh air hit me, refreshing me and reviving me a little. A few of the lads from the other Blocks stood there, their faces as white as ghosts, as white as the snow they stood on, awaiting their turn, no doubt having heard the yells and thuds of my fate and knowing only too well that it was to be their fate next.

'Okay, Bobby?' one of the lads asked.

I couldn't answer. I nodded in recognition and sympathy, thinking of where they were going and took consolation from the relieving fact that at least I had the torturous ordeal behind me. I trudged onwards towards the H-Block. There was no van about and I was only too glad of the short walk, gorging myself in the luxury of a few minutes of fresh, clean air. That's the worst and first hurdle over, I thought.

The road ahead of me was wide and white with snow. It hung on the dull grey timbers and clung to the miles of tangled, gruesome barbed wire. There was fencing and barbed wire everywhere. A jungle of it flanked at intervals by looming sinister camouflaged gun posts where armed British soldiers scanned the camp from perimeter to perimeter. It reminded me of a clip of film I once saw, when I was young, of a Nazi concentration camp in winter and I remember, although young, feeling shocked but also secure in my chair by the fire, thinking that that type of place was a horror of the past and could not nor ever would be allowed or tolerated again, least of all in Ireland and never upon me.

I thought of families whispering together around the tables of the visiting room, the faces of mothers lined with sorrow, speechless fathers and crying, whimpering children watching their daddies being bundled away by the monsters in black uniforms, the same heartless monsters who hung over your shoulder listening to every word and syllable spoken, who kept your people queuing for hours on end for a half hour visit, herding them about like cattle through one gate to the next, through one degrading, humiliating search to another, treating them like animals.

They despised our people as much as they despised and hated us. They insulted them, harassed them and broke their hearts by torturing their sons and daughters. I was naïve when I was young. Here I was now going back to a filthy concrete tomb to fight for my survival, to fight for my right to be recognised as a political Prisoner-of-War, a right for which I would never stop fighting.

The H-Block loomed up ahead of me on my right. I stood waiting for the gate to open — the gate to hell. A sinister silence reigned: not so much as a sigh from the wind stirred, not one bird sang but there was nothing in Belsen to sing about either, I thought, going through the gate to hell.

I walked across the yard to the front door of the H-Block. On my left the boys in the other wing were standing at their windows. The lights were on in a few cells. The rest of the cells were in darkness. Those cells with the lights on looked like little caves, the inhabitants wrapped up in their shabby blankets. They were scary-looking, their long beards and pale faces peering out at me from behind the concrete bars.

I could see the slight movements of shadowy figures in the cells that were in darkness.

'All right, Bobby?' one of the boys shouted. I couldn't answer so I waved back, feeling a little stupid.

'Won't be long now!' someone else shouted and the boys began joking and slagging out the windows. I looked to my right at the other leg of the H, which was my wing. There were no windows, not even a shadow of light to be seen. The entire outside length of the wing was shrouded with the corrugated iron and timber structure which blocked out all light and view of the outside. Thank God they haven't got around to my side of the wing yet, I thought. But they would soon!

I entered the Block and stood waiting at the iron grill gates, my unwanted barking escort disappearing. I was passed from one grill to the next until 'A—' appeared and admitted me back into my wing again. The high-pitched whining, droning noise of the machine which was sucking up the pools of urine still lying upon the corridor was echoing around the wing. The tea-trolley was parked outside the search cell. I passed by it, noticing the coat of slimy skin that had formed upon the freezing cold tea. The slices of bread were piled high, and were curled up and stale. The food lay on the plates. A piece of meat that represented a beef burger was almost surrounded, but not quite, by twenty or so beans.

I walked on into the search cell, all thoughts of food disappearing in a flash as I saw 'C—' and 'D—' standing there. Walking ahead of my escort from the visit I had been able to move the parcel about in my mouth and swallow my spittle but my throat was now parched again. I began to strip the clothes off me — two minutes and I would be safe. Just two more minutes! I took the trousers off and wrapped the towel around me again. I'd no sooner had it around me when 'D—' said, 'Drop your towel and turn round!' I was waiting for the bending-over bit. I dropped my towel and turned around but to my surprise nothing came. I grabbed my towel and rewrapped it around me, making for the cell entrance. That was it. I've made it or I haven't! I walked on out the door still waiting for the words that would hail discovery, but they never came. I could barely believe my luck. 'A—' sniggered at me and said, 'You'd be as well to take your tea back to your cell with you in case it gets cold.'

'C—' and 'D—' found that very amusing. The hovering orderlies went into hysterics. I ignored them and took the plate and cup noticing the meagre contents.

I walked on down the wing which by now was dry at the end where I was walking. The screw with the machine was still working away at the far end and was almost finished. The drone was mind-wrecking. I was as happy as a lark. I couldn't wait to get back into my cell. I dreaded the thought but it was purely to be able to spit out my well-travelled contraband. 'A—' opened the door and I stepped back into the darkness of my filthy cold tomb. The door slammed behind me and I stood in the darkness.

Victory!

I wished I could have told them that I had outdone them, that I had put one over on them, especially that bastard 'C—'. I could hardly believe that I had made it back safely.

Yahoo!

I set my cold tea on the floor and took the parcel out of my mouth. It was a relief. The wee parcel was wet and I dried it on the end of my towel. I couldn't examine it in the darkness. I would do that later. I wrapped the three blankets around me and put my wee parcel in the fold of the blanket that was wrapped around my waist. The doors were opening and slamming shut as the cold tea was being handed into the cells. The drone of the cleaning machine continued unabated and they'd probably leave it on for a few hours to try and drive us insane. I wondered had anything else occurred while I was away. I threw the cold tea out the window and took a quick look into the corners where the rubbish lay, just in case an adventurous rat had decided to have a look around while I was out. It wouldn't have been the first time that that had happened to me; it even happened during the night on one occasion. I sat down on the mattress and began to eat my cold food, reflecting on the highlight of my month, my visit. I finished off my cold, meagre tea and set the plastic dishes at the door. Back to my fight for survival, I thought, feeling the cold and rising to resume where I had left off on my endless walk to nowhere in the darkness. I checked that my little parcel was secure and revelled in the self-esteem of success. I couldn't figure out why 'C—' and 'D—' didn't try to forcibly bend me over when I arrived back to carry out another humiliating body search. They had seemed somewhat eager to get me back to my cell again.

The floor was very cold so I stopped to spread a blanket on it to enable me to continue my endless pacing. The snow still lay on the ground outside and began to fall again slowly, little flakes floating in through the open window. The cleaning machine, deliberately left on, droned in the background. I tried to overcome the harassing sound with thought. I would have liked to tell Seán the good news of the victory, but he wouldn't hear me with the continuous noise. I began to think about the wee bits of *scéal* that I had heard on my visit to tell the boys later on. It wouldn't be long until supper time for the tea had been served very late but that wouldn't be anything to look forward to either — probably a mug of lukewarm tea and a round of bread and margarine. All it really meant was that it wouldn't be long until lock-up when the screws would go home for the night and no more cell doors would open until tomorrow morning.

I gazed out the window thinking that I could always watch the rats running up and down the yard when it got really quiet later on. I wouldn't be able to get into my bed on the ground too early. The cold wouldn't allow me to sleep. I was tired; in fact I was exhausted but the day was not over yet by any means. I wondered how the boys on the boards were. Perhaps someone in another Block or wing may have come back from the boards today and could tell if anything else had occurred. The shouting to the other wings and Blocks would start when things settled down later, when the screws went home.

I heard the slam of the cell door facing me. It had been barely audible. They were probably collecting the dishes. No use shouting out the door with the drone, as no one would hear it.

My cell door opened and the light was turned on. The orderly lifted the dishes and the door slammed shut again. I didn't see the screws as the illumination of the cell left me temporarily blinded. The sudden change from darkness to light cut at my eyes. My stinking surroundings came screaming up at me once again. The white squares of discarded stale bread added a new feature to the rubbish piles in the corners. I noticed the marks in the sides of the slices of bread and lifted one from the rubbish. It was blue-moulded. Thank God I hadn't eaten the bread, I thought, examining the rest of the slices to find that they were the same. I knew immediately what had happened, why 'C—' and 'D—' didn't forcibly bend me over and why they were so eager to get me back to my cell to eat my tea in the dark. I had been too busy thinking of my mouth full of contraband to scrutinise the bread on my plate on my way back to the cell.

The cleaning machine droned and whined in the background. The cell light was very bright and already my eyes were hurting. I felt the dreaded early warning tinges of a migraine headache building up inside the back of my head. I kept pacing the floor, taking deep breaths of air at the window to try and clear the stuffy, wheezy sickliness that was also beginning to bother me. The machine became more annoying. The temperature was falling outside and the coating of frost on the wire grew thicker. I took out my little parcel and had a peek at it. It was intact. I could see the contents through the 'stretch and seal' plastic wrapping, the wee note, the cigarette papers and the brown tobacco. I couldn't open it up now so I put it back again in the fold of my blanket for later. Being the possessor of a wee note from my sister, cigarette papers and a quarter ounce of tobacco made me feel like a king.

What would it be like if they were to open the door now and throw me out to freedom? I wouldn't be able to cope with it. Dear God! I could hardly bear up to a visit. I just couldn't imagine what state I would be in if I were to be released from this torture. I knew how to appreciate small, seemingly unimportant things now that one time or another I would have taken for granted or probably not even noticed. When was the last time I received a decent warm meal? Funny how one can adapt to things — especially when you are starving, I thought, remembering the times during the summer when the orderlies and screws had dropped maggots into our dinners and all we could do was search for them and remove them, then eat our dinners as if nothing had happened. It was either that or starve!

The drone from the cleaning machine suddenly

stopped and a terrible unnatural silence fell once again. I heard the footsteps of the screw who had turned off the machine returning back along the wing. I put my eye to the little spy-hole. It was 'A—'. He walked on past towards the little office. I heard the sound of the television going but was unable to make out any words. The orderlies were shouting and carrying on between themselves. I heard 'C—' shouting, 'Right,' and the carry on of the shouting orderlies died immediately to be replaced by the rattle of the tea-trolley.

'Tea on the air,' some of the lads shouted in Gaelic. The cell doors began to open and close. They passed by my cell going down the other side of the wing. One of the lads a few cells down was singing to himself and a bit of life came back into the wing. The tea-trolley finally arrived at my door. The usual hated faces were standing there when the cell door opened. The orderly handed me a mug of tea and a slice of bread doubled in two. I caught 'D—' sniggering as he saw me glancing at the bread for any signs of blue mould. It was all right.

The door slammed and I retreated to the mattress detecting an unnatural warmth and seeing the steam rising from the plastic mug. It was hot! I could hardly believe it. I sat down and somewhat sheepishly tasted it. It was as weak as water. In fact it was simply coloured hot water, but I decided to brave it. Anything hot was a Godsend on a night like this, I thought, even hot water. I ate the slice of bread and sipped the warm weak tea. It won't be long until lock-

up, I thought, relishing the thought of the parcel and the smoke.

My mother and father and sister would be at home now and most likely they wouldn't be feeling the best. They would have had a terrible hard day and having seen my appearance they would do nothing else but worry. I thought of the families who had two or three sons inside and those with sons on the blanket protest, or those with daughters on protest in Armagh. It must be really hard on those families. There was heartbreak everywhere. That's all that ever came out of the stinking hell holes — heartbreak and grief.

I couldn't drink any more of the weak tea. It was growing cooler and becoming a bit sickening. I rose and threw it out the window upon the snow and watched the puff of steam rise as it buried itself into the snow. Setting the cup at the door I returned to my pacing as the doors began to open and close.

'Cups off the air,' came the cry.

My feet were getting colder. I stamped them on the blanket on the floor. The cold was going to be very intense tonight all right. The singer down the wing began to sing a new song to himself. There was nothing to sing about but one had to overcome the terrible monotony some way or other. I was getting bored myself but it was more impatience than anything else as my wee parcel was burning a hole in my blanket so to speak.

My cell door opened and the cup was removed. I didn't even bother to look round. The door slammed and the procession of screws and orderlies proceeded towards the end of the wing. I sat down on the mattress once again to rest. There were eight of the boys on the other side of the wing who smoked, plus nine on this side, but three were away to the boards, so that left fourteen smokers, including myself. I would be able to manage a cigarette for everyone tonight with perhaps a bit to spare. It would mean shooting a line under the bottom of the best door across the wing to the cells opposite to get the cigarettes over to the other lads. The boys on the other side of the wing couldn't swing or pass things out of their windows because they were blocked up. But they had engineered little holes in the walls where the pipes ran through which would enable them to pass the cigarettes up and down the line, as well as a light. A light for the cigarettes would be engineered by one of the lads using a piece of glass, a small flint and a wee bit of fluffy wool. A wick would be made and lit, allowing the glowing material to be passed carefully from one cell to the next, until everyone got a light. Getting a line across would be tricky and dangerous. It always was. The screws knew we did it and they were always on the prowl, lurking and tiptoeing around the wing at night. 'B—' would be on tonight, on night-guard, which meant that we would have to be extra careful. I checked to see if the long line that I had plaited earlier was still there. It was all right.

Seán knocked on the wall.

'Down to the pipe,' I said, getting down to the corner on top of my mattress with my head right to the wall where the pipes ran through. There wasn't a great deal of heat coming through the pipes. What there was went streaming out the open window into the dark cold night.

'Well, Bobby,' came Seán's enquiring voice through the small hole in the wall.

'*Go h-an mhaith*, Seán,' I said in delight. 'I made it back with the other.' He knew what I meant.

'*Maith thú*,' he said, and I began to tell him about my visit and related the happenings with the searches and all the rest. I sensed the excitement building up in Seán's voice as I told about all the happenings, the great turn out for the parade and the massive offensive in the war effort. In general things were going better than ever before. The British government's attempts to criminalise the Republican Movement had failed miserably and now everyone realised just exactly what the motive behind the tortures in the H-Blocks were aimed at. I continued my conversation with Seán for some time until I began to feel cramped lying in my unnatural position at the pipes and wall. So I decided to go back to pacing the floor once again. My feet were numb with the cold. Seán understood. He was in much the same condition. I told him that I'd call him later and we both left our corners to resume where we had left off in our endless pacing.

The screws began to lock grills and doors in preparation for the nearing lock-up. The orderlies had left the wing for their dormitories which were two large rooms adjoining the wings especially opened and equipped with such luxuries as television, radio and record player and a host of other things: the payment for their dirty work that they did exceedingly well. Some orderlies didn't bother us but they were very few and hard to find.

'A—', 'C—' and 'D—' were hovering at the top of the wing talking and joking and waiting on the call to lock up. It couldn't be too far away, I thought, perhaps fifteen minutes. There were two head counts to be done yet. One by the leaving screws, 'A—' and company, and the other by the night-guard who would be arriving shortly. The night-guard would only consist of four screws. Sometimes they watched television, played cards or drank themselves into a stupor and wouldn't bother us. But most times there was trouble and more so if there was someone like 'B—' on. And 'B—' was on tonight!

I was bored pacing up and down so I decided to sit down and risk opening my wee parcel. The chances of a cell search now were slender but the danger was always there so one had to be very careful. It would be a terrible thing to get caught after what I had gone through today but I was impatient to get reading my wee note, so I took out my little treasured parcel and began peeling the glossy 'stretch and seal' off it until I had the note. Before I began to read my sister's letter, I wrapped the loose 'stretch and seal' back around the rest of the contents, just in case. I sat quietly for two or three minutes taking in every word of her neat handwriting. When I had finished I re-read it. It was good to hear from her again. It seemed an eternity since I had seen her but she seemed to be doing all right, more worried about me than anything else and enquiring about the other lads that she knew. I would have to try and get a wee note to her as soon as I could. We had one miserly pencil and a pen refill that were constantly in use around the wing, going from one cell to the next, back and forth from one side of the wing to the other, eating up sheets of 'bog roll' (toilet paper) for the wee smuggled notes to worried wives, mothers and girl-friends; for the letters to the newspapers and the quickly scribbled notes to the H-Block Information Bureau telling of the beatings and horrors that took place every single day. I would have to wait my turn for the pen or pencil.

I tore my sister's wee note up into shreds and threw it out the open window watching it blow across the snow-covered yard until it disappeared along with the falling snow. 'A—' and company were still at the top of the wing at the grills. I could hear the jingling of the keys and the occasional murmuring voice. I decided to take another chance and open the parcel once again to roll the cigarettes and have them ready for the lads and the line to be shot across the wing later. I unwrapped the covering again and took out the small lump of tobacco that was very fresh and squashed for convenience sake. I began to shred it and loosen it up to enable me to roll the cigarettes. The small lump grew into a small stringy pile. The aroma of the tobacco was a pleasant change from the evil stench that usually hung in the air of my cell. I stripped the cigarette papers that clung to each other into a pile until I had enough for my requirements and a few left over. When I had everything ready I commenced my task of rolling them, my ears alert for the slightest tell-tale sound of a footstep or key, while telling myself all the time that it wouldn't be long until I was lying on the mattress smoking one of the cigarettes that I was making now.

Five completed! I began the sixth, thinking how much one lousy cigarette meant and how it could lift morale, even of the lads who didn't smoke. Somehow or other everybody realised and took satisfaction from the fact that somebody or other had gotten one over on the bastards like 'A—' and 'C—' and that meant a great deal. I lifted another cigarette paper to begin the seventh cigarette. . .

'Bears in the air.'

I heard the jingle of a key and whipped the blanket over the contraband as the lock on my door rattled and the door flew open. I tried to act normally in my panic, shock flooding my entire body. 'A—' looked into the cell.

'One,' he said as 'C—' slammed the door shut again.

'Head count on the air,' I yelled, terror clinging to my voice.

'Two,' I heard 'A—' say as Seán's door slammed.

'Four, six, eight,' as they continued down the wing.

A cold wave swept my body. That was close, I thought, as I looked at the blanket that covered the tobacco and cigarettes. One cigarette was half visible, but they never saw it. I sat glued to my mattress as the head count continued.

'Twenty, twenty-two, twenty-four, twenty-six. . .'
'A—' counted.

'Bears off the air,' one of the lads shouted, signalling the all-clear as the final number tallied and 'A—', 'C—' and 'D—' left the wing slamming the office door shut as they departed. I recovered my composure and contraband and went back to my rolling. I should have everything finished before the next and last head count I thought. Besides we'd hear 'B—' long before he'd even reach the wing, as he would most certainly be drunk. I worked on until I had completed all the cigarettes whereupon I divided them into two parcels. One contained the cigarettes for the lads on the other side, and the other one contained a cigarette each for the boys down this side.

I got the long, thin line that I had plaited earlier and tied both parcels to it and attached a bit of stale blue moulded bread to the end of it to weight it before rapping on the wall for Séan.

'Hello,' he shouted.

'Put your hand out,' I said and began swinging the line to him. When he caught hold of it I explained the contents of the parcels telling him to send the line and the parcel down the wing to the man who would be doing the shot to the other side so that he could get things ready. Seán knocked on the cell wall next to him and began to get things boxed off with the lads. I put my own cigarette, plus an extra one for myself and Seán, under the pillow.

The rattle of grills and keys sounded, then footsteps followed by a mouthful of obscenities as 'B—'

announced his arrival. The footsteps came tramping down the wing and the final head count began on the other side of the wing to another barrage of slamming doors. They worked their way around the doors and then my door opened. 'B——' peered in. He was barely able to stand let alone count. He half stumbled away and the door shut again.

'Bears off the air.' The all-clear came. No one had even bothered to announce their arrival. It was obvious enough. A hush fell upon the wing and one of the men down the wing called out, 'Right lads, we'll say the Rosary now. Who is going to say the first mystery?'

'I will,' someone shouted.

'And the second?'

'I will,' said Seán, and three other lads volunteered to say the three remaining decades.

'It's the sorrowful mysteries tonight,' the same voice said, blessing himself and saying the opening prayers himself. The Rosary continued being answered by the boys out the doors. Mid-way through the third mystery a screw decided to bang the grills with his baton. The Rosary carried on and as usual the screw got fed up and departed. When the Rosary ended the wing was a flurry of activity and buzzing with conversation.

The boys down the wing decided to do the line across the wing before 'B——' came prowling or some other screw.

'Hey, Bobby. Will you keep watch?' one of the boys shouted.

'Okay. Go ahead,' I shouted back, going to my little spy-hole at the door.

Shooting the line across would be a tricky operation.

'Hey, Seán, can you see out your door?' the same voice asked.

'No way,' Seán answered.

'I can,' one of the lads at the bottom said.

'Can you see Gerard's door?'

'No problem,' came the reply.

'*Maith thú,*' said the man who was about to do the shot. 'You can guide us.'

'You there, Bobby?' someone asked, double checking. If the line was caught it would be a catastrophe.

'I'm here,' I said, not daring to move my eye from the little hole. The long line would be secured to a button and flicked along the ground under the door and across the corridor. The man on the other side would search for it outside his door, using a strip of paper. When he detected it he would slide the paper underneath it and pull it in under his door. Then the ferrying of notes, cigarettes or whatever, to and fro began! The cigarettes would be tied on to the line and like a long train dragged across.

'You ready, Gerard?' the shooter asked.

'Go ahead, Pat,' came the reply. There was a sharp crack and the scrape of the button sliding across the floor.

'Can you see it, Brian?' the shooter asked the man guiding him down the wing a bit.

'Too far to the left,' he said. 'Shoot it again.'

The line was drawn in and the sharp crack sounded again as the button slid across the corridor. The wing was deadly silent, every ear listening for the slightest tell-tale sound.

'What's that like, Brian?'

'Too short,' came the tense reply.

The line was drawn in once again. The third shot was too hard and bounced off the door and had to be tried again. The fourth sharp crack sounded.

'How's that?' came the nervous voice of the shooter. The whole wing listened in anticipation.

'Leave it where it is,' came the excited reply.

'Put your piece of paper out, Gerard,' the spotter directed.

The paper rustled as it slid out underneath.

'Move it to the left,' he directed again. 'Another few inches. That's it. Leave it there. Now, push it out as far as you can. No good. Try it again.'

My eye was beginning to hurt being pressed against the little hole. The silence remained. No one dared to speak except the team at work. The paper rustled again.

'Push it on out, Gerard, nice and gently. That's it! Easy, easy! *Maith thú,* Gerard. The button's sitting on top of the paper. Pull it back in to you slowly! Go ahead, go ahead! Take it easy.'

'I've got it,' came the successful disclosure.

'All right up there, Bobby?'

'Okay. I think so anyway, Pat.'

'Pull the line on over in to you, Gerard,' Pat said, 'but don't tug too hard.'

The cigarettes slid out underneath the shooter's door and across the corridor.

'Take it easy,' the spotter said, 'or they will stick underneath the door.'

All the cigarettes got under Gerard's door except the last one which got entangled in the line.

'Don't pull it,' Brian said. 'Flick the line a little. That's it. It's sorting itself out. Try it now,' he said. I caught a glimpse of a moving shadow and the squeak of a boot.

'Bear in the air!' I yelled as he shot past my line of vision.

'Pull it on in, Gerard!' Brian yelled. There was a scuffling noise as the screw tried to grab the line. Then silence followed by the retreating footsteps of the screw. I caught a glimpse of his face as he passed by. He was a stranger.

'All right, Gerard?' Pat asked.

'Okay, Pat. I got all the "blows" in but the screw got the button.' At least the cigrettes were okay. The loss of the button wasn't a catastrophe but a loss all the same in these conditions.

'Okay, lads. Slop out now,' the O/C said. We began to filter the reeking urine out the doors. If we didn't do it then the screws would do it for us first thing in the morning. It's not a pleasant thing to be awakened by the splashing contents of a filthy po of urine! There wasn't too much left in the pos due to the slop out earlier on. I worked at the foot of the door trying to get it out. When I'd finished I retreated to the mattress to rest. I was completely out of breath and panting, a good indication of just how bad a state my physical health is in, I thought, when I became exhausted that easily. I sat back awaiting the arrival of the glowing wick which would provide me with a light. Lucky enough with the 'blows', I thought. If the screw had arrived a few minutes earlier he would have caught the whole lot. Seán knocked on the wall.

'Right, Bobby, here's the effort.'

I knew what he meant and I put my hand out the window to catch the swinging line with the glowing, improvised wick dangling at the end of it. I took it in and lit my cigarette.

'Here you are, Seán,' I called.

'Go ahead,' he answered, as I swung the line back into him. He knocked on the other wall to pass it down the line again as I lay down to smoke the cigarette. It was soothing and a relief to lie and enjoy something without the worry of the door bursting open. The keys for the doors were not kept in the H-Blocks but elsewhere. The boys in the other wing would see the arrival of any strange screws bearing keys and raise the alarm.

'Bears in the yard,' came the warning, but there was no real need for concern unless you were in the process of swinging something to another cell. The screws were down at the bottom of the yard hurling abuse at the lads further down. I finished off my cigarette then I got up to the window to see who they were. They came swaggering up the yard, 'B—' was shouting and slobbering his head off. There were two others along with him who were endeavouring to add their fourpence worth of abuse. They passed on by in the direction of the other wing. The O/C called for everyone's attention and silence fell immediately as he asked did anyone see or make out what happened during the earlier incidents concerning the slop out and Pee Wee O'Donnell. I told him what I had heard and seen out the door. Several others were able to put more to it. He then asked what were the injuries received during the early morning wing shift. The bloody accounts of damage were given out the doors.

'Okay,' he said when everyone had finished. 'Nothing else?' That was all the business concluded and noted for the Information Centre outside.

'Any *scéal*, Bobby?' some of the lads asked and for about five minutes I related all that I had heard.

'I think that's the heap, lads,' I said, when I was certain I had yelled it all out.

'Yahoos' and 'yahoos' and cheers followed. Then the conversations at the windows, pipes and doors resumed, discussing, debating and speculating upon every little piece of news. The *scéal* was good and that meant a terrible lot. Reports were coming across the far yard to the lads whose windows were blocked up from the other wing about what had taken place that day in the other two wings of the Block. One man from each wing was away to the boards. One man was beaten up very badly, six cells hosed down and the daily horror reports kept coming in. The stench from the outside corridor was sickening. I rose and moved to the window to try and get some air. The snow glistened in the brilliance of the mass of lights and the noise of shouting and singing came on the breeze from the other blanket blocks. Hundreds of naked, physically wrecked men had come alive. It was bitter cold now. I wrapped all the blankets around me and put the towel around my head like a scarf once more. The boys in the other blocks were shouting to each other, passing messages back and forth and the horror reports began to be shouted from the other blocks. Several men severely beaten during a wing shift. Two men taken to the boards. Three men scalded in another wing and two men sent to the boards having been caught with tobacco coming back from visits. One man returned from the boards and had been beaten up and forcibly bathed while he was there. Several men beaten up and forcibly bathed on the boards. Pee Wee O'Donnell taken to the hospital, and the others badly bruised.

'You hear that, Seán?' I said.

'I heard it, Bobby,' he answered. The horror reports continued: forty-four men beaten, bathed and had their heads shaved in another wing; two men in hospital and two more missing, probably on the boards. The reports in Gaelic continued. H5 began to tell H3 that several men were hurt during a slop out done by the screws and one man was taken to the boards. H3 received six new blanket-men sentenced the day before. The shouting continued. The distance to each block was quite a bit but the sound echoed and carried in the night across the snow over the grey timbers and barbed wire. Several messages had to be repeated before they were understood and several times words had to be spelled out a letter at a time. But with a bit of perseverence and patience the communications system worked. But with the blocking up of the windows that would finish also!

'Lights out,' one of the boys shouted on the other side of the wing. The screws were extinguishing the lights. They'd most likely be around in the middle of the night to put them on again; not that we'd get much sleep with the cold anyway, I thought, as the screw put my light out. I knocked on the wall for Seán.

'Hello,' he said.

'Get the effort up the line,' I said.

'*Maith thú,*' he replied and called up the line for the improvised wick.

'Are you listening, Seán?' I asked and added, 'I'll swing you in a "blow" when I'm sending the line back again. Okay?'

'*Maith thú,*' he replied once again.

The line reached Seán's cell and he swung it in to me, whereupon I lit the second cigarette, tied on the one for him and swung it back to him again.

'Okay, comrade?'

'Sound,' he replied.

I sat down once again. I kept thinking that the chances I had taken had been worth it. The smoke streamed upwards in the dim light and out the windows and for another few minutes the stench was blotted out by the aroma of tobacco. It was very cold. I decided to go back to my pacing when I had finished my cigarette. Poor Pee Wee, I thought, lying in the prison hospital or maybe even in Musgrave! The rest of the lads on the boards would be lying battered and sore. I wasn't feeling the best myself. My earlier wounds grew more and more painful but I knew that I was a lot better off than the boys on the boards. I watched the reddened ash of the cigarette die on the blackened floor and I rose once more to walk the floor for another while, carpeting the floor with one of the blankets.

'Bears in the yard!' came drifting across from one of the other Blocks. It was really cold now and the snow lay deeper in the yard and continued to fall steadily. I wondered what the torture-mongers would be doing now. 'A—' would most likely be sitting drinking in the screws' club in the camp with the rest of his mercenary friends and Brit soldiers; 'C—' and 'D—' would be in their houses with their families and I wondered what they'd say if their children asked them, 'What did you do today, Daddy?' Or better still, what would their wives and children say if they knew what they did and just how much suffering, grief and torture they were causing and perpetrating upon hundreds of naked men?

I paced onwards in my endless circles to nowhere. The lads were still talking and joking, one or two singing and humming to themselves. I was about to sit down once more upon my mattress when the warning shout rang out.

'Bears in the air! Heavy gear!'

I knew just what that meant. I dived at the mattress and put it standing lengthways, in the farthest corner from the door, against the wall and put all the blankets behind it, wrapping the towel around my waist, forgetting the cold and securing the remains of my little tobacco parcel in the waist band of the towel. I heard the first splash of lashing liquid at the cell facing me.

Heavy gear, all right! I could smell it already: ammonia-based detergent, a very strong and extremely dangerous disinfectant. The screws were lashing it in under and through the splits in the sides of the doors. I braved a quick glance through my little spy-hole as the lights in the corridor were turned on. It was a very foolish and dangerous thing to do because if the disinfectant hit me in the eyes it would burn my eyes out, blind me in a matter of seconds. 'B—' was lashing a full bucket of the sickening liquid in under the door facing me and shouting to the other screws to hurry up and fetch more. I heard the chokes and coughs of the man across from me. The boys on the other side of the wing were in trouble. Their windows were blocked up. The fumes from the disinfectant were similar to tear gas, they cut at the eyes and throat, bringing on fits of vomiting and temporary blindness. I heard the hose being unravelled at the top of the wing.

'Hose on the air,' I yelled and stepped back from the door. 'B—' was lashing the disinfectant in through the doors like a mad man, laughing all the while. He had been wearing a small face-mask which protected him from the fumes and no doubt he and his companions were clad in their blue nylon overalls. The hose burst into life and the thundering jets crashed against the bottom of the doors. I heard a swish and saw the greenish coloured liquid flooding in under the door. Immediately the terrible fumes struck me and I began coughing and spluttering, my eyes watering as I made my way to the window. My stomach was turning and I thought I was going to be sick as I fought for gasps of air at the window, my head pressed tightly against the concrete bars. Every single man must have been at his window coughing. That's all I could hear with the swish of the high-powered hose in the background. The tears were tripping me. I couldn't see a thing. Then the water came pouring in the sides of the door and came flooding across the blackened floor. I couldn't have cared less. I was shattered and coughing, my throat burning and dry. The water would dilute the disinfectant. I knew that. But it would be several minutes before the fumes cleared. The water from the hose was still streaming in under the door then it ceased as the screw moved on to another cell. I was still coughing and spluttering but the fumes were clearing. I could hear Seán vomiting violently. The whole wing was filled with moans and groans and coughing. 'B—' was literally screaming, 'See how yous like that. See how yous like that.' Then he began singing the only song he knew — *The Sash*.

The screws turned the hose off. I braved it to the spy-hole to see 'B—' plodding through the river of water, disinfectant and urine with his face-mask in one hand and an empty bucket in the other. He was laughing like a madman. The other screw came behind him, dragging the deflated hose, whilst the third screw hurled obscenities and abuse from the end of the wing. My eyes were burning but I wasn't too bad. The coughing still went on in the other cells. There was at least an inch of water on the floor, the end of my mattress was submerged in it, but the blankets were safely tucked in behind the mattress on the pipes. I began the long exhausting job of scraping and pushing the ocean of liquid out under the door as best I could.

'All right, Seán?' I yelled.

'No! I'm shattered!' he answered. The coughing in the other cells died out to be replaced by the noise of scraping pos as the drying-up operation began. The stinking, putrifying rubbish was floating about around my feet and clogging whatever little gap there was at the bottom of my door. I had to keep clearing it with my hand, lifting handfuls of soggy bread, dirt and filth and flinging them back into the corner. The water level began to subside. The fumes of the disinfectant still hung in the air but they were mild. I glanced at the window. The snow was falling really heavy now and a soft breeze was directing it in through the window.

Dear God, I thought, what next? My feet were numb and soaking but my exhausted body was sweating as I continued to scrape and push the water out. When I had most of it out, I took the mattress and tried to squeeze the water out of the saturated part at the bottom of it. Then I tore a lump off it and began to soak up the remaining damp patches on the floor, leaving the soaking end of the mattress against the pipes in the hope that it would dry out. I took another peek out of my little spy-hole and gazed at the river of urine and filth and everything else that lay like a lake outside in the wing. They'd be around in the middle of the night with the cleaning machine to clean and dry it all up. I threw the damp piece of foam into the corner and stood at the window to catch my breath. I was exhausted but I couldn't stand too long on the freezing cold floor. The snow flakes were still coming in through the window. I had still only the towel wrapped around me so I lifted the blankets and wrapped myself up again. The floor was still slimy and damp. I would have no alternative but to put the mattress down on it later knowing that the dampness would seep up through the foam and attack my body. But it was either that or walk all night which I wouldn't be able to do. It was going to be a long, freezing cold restless night. I listened to the boys describing their predicament out the windows. Several of the lads' mattresses were completely saturated. The blankets of others were in the same state. I wasn't too bad. At least it was only the lower end of my bed that was wet.

All the noise had died and mattresses and blankets were being dried as best they could. 'Does anyone fancy a sing-song?' came the familiar question. After what had just occurred we had to do something to bolster our morale, and besides everyone would be pacing the floor. A bit of a cheer went up and the first singer was called to a roar of applause. I paced back and forth listening to the first singer singing *The Old Alarm Clock*. The next singer was one of the Derry lads. He sang *My Old Home Town on the Foyle*, and after that the singers kept stepping up to their doors as they were called. Then came my call and I braved it to the door to give my rendering of *The Curragh of Kildare* and all the while, as I sang, I was waiting for 'B—' to return and slip up unnoticed to lash a bucket of disinfectant into my face through the side of the door. I finished my song, being somewhat breathless, to a round of applause and went back to my pacing as the next singer was called. My feet were numb. The floor had dried very little and was still slimy. I couldn't walk any more, so I threw my mattress back onto the ground and crouched up in the corner on the dry half of it. The bruises I had received in the wing shift and search outside the visits were hurting.

I was tempted to roll another cigarette for myself and Seán but I decided against it as I knew I might well be able to manage one 'blow' between two down the line tomorrow night and the way things were going it most likely would be more than welcome then. The singing continued. It broke the monotony and the tension-filled air and for a few minutes helped to take your mind off your surroundings and situation. There was no sign of 'B—' returning. Most likely he was lying on his back around in the screws' mess or else filling himself with more booze. Someone was singing a self-composed song about the blanket-men which was very good indeed. Then one of the lads began to sing *Ashtown Road*. The wing went deadly silent and I sat, slightly shivering, listening to every note and word of the beautiful rendering as the singer sang on in his very sad voice. I felt my morale rising and once again I was glad I was resisting. Better suffering while resisting than being tortured without fighting back at all. The singer finished and the lads nearly tore the place down. The Master of Ceremonies called on the same singer to sing the last song and away he went again with *The Wind that Shakes the Barley*.

The snow was still coming in the paneless window which reminded me of the night when we had to smash them with our bare hands when the screws lashed gallons of the heavy disinfectant in through the doors. The lads on the other side must have got it really bad tonight. I had heard them cursing the blocked up windows when 'B—' had lashed the disinfectant through their doors.

The singer finished the last song of the night, and everyone gave him a grand round of applause. A bit of chatter followed and someone on the other side was getting a message shouted over in Gaelic from the other wing, which was passed on to the O/C. Some lad was very sick in the other wing. They rang the bell and the screws turned the emergency bell off and ignored the sick man. Another lad's mother had died yesterday and he had been refused parole like all the rest who had been in the same sorrowful position before him.

I got to my feet and stood on the mattress gazing out the window once more. The frost was thick on the wire which sort of reminded me of the inside of a 'fridge. Some of the boys down below were saying goodnight to each other; others were saying that they were going to try and walk as long as possible as their mattresses were soaking. Only a few remained talking at the windows. Seán knocked on the wall.

'*Óiche mhaith,* Bobby,' he shouted.

'*Óiche mhaith,* Seán,' I replied and added, 'is your mattress wet?'

'No, it's not too bad,' he replied. 'I'm going to try and get warm under the blankets.'

'*Maith thú. Óiche mhaith, a chara,*' I said.

'*Óiche mhaith,*' he shouted again.

The snow had stopped falling and only a soft breeze blew. The once smooth untarnished surface of the snow was marred by the footprints of the screws. The white puffy snow clouds had forsaken the sky and the inky-black sky returned, bearing a few stars that twinkled here and there. Most people would be in bed now, I thought. I wonder how they would feel if they had to wake up to what lies in front of us tomorrow? Is it any wonder, I ask myself, that I've had several nightmares this past few weeks and everyone of them connected with this hell-hole. Dear God, where is it all going to end? It's bad when you can't even escape it through sleep, I thought.

The noise had died completely in the other blocks and those who had remained at the windows drifted away to either sleep or stay up because of the state of their mattresses. It was very quiet. The snow glinted and glistened as the multi-coloured brilliant lights reflected on it. The silence was ugly and sinister. A curlew cried out in the darkness as it passed overhead. The spotlight of a hovering helicopter danced about in the black ocean of sky far in the distance and I wondered if my family were all right. They would be worried sick until another month's visit came around. It had been a hard day but wasn't every day the same and God only knew what tomorrow would bring. Who would be the unlucky unfortunates tomorrow, supplying the battered bloody bodies for the punishment block? Who would be hosed down, beaten up or torn apart during a wing shift? Tomorrow would only bring more pain and torture and suffering, boredom and fear and God knows how many humiliations, inhumanities and horrors. Darkness and intense cold, an empty stomach and the four screaming walls of a filthy nightmare-filled tomb to remind me of my plight, that's what lay ahead tomorrow for hundreds of naked Republican Political Prisoners-of-War, but just as sure as the morrow would be filled with torture so would we carry on and remain unbroken. It was hard, it was very, very hard, I thought, lying down upon my damp mattress and pulling the blankets around me. But some day victory would be ours and never again would another Irish man or woman rot in an English hell-hole.

It was cold, so very, very cold. I rolled on to my side and placed my little treasured piece of tobacco under the mattress and felt the dampness clinging to my feet.

That's another day nearer to victory, I thought,

feeling very hungry.

I was a skeleton compared to what I used to be but it didn't matter. Nothing really mattered except remaining unbroken. I rolled over once again, the cold biting at me. They have nothing in their entire imperial arsenal to break the spirit of one single Republican Political Prisoner-of-War who refuses to be broken, I thought, and that was very true. They can not or never will break our spirit. I rolled over again freezing and the snow came in the window on top of my blankets.

'Tiocfaidh ár lá,' * I said to myself. *'Tiocfaidh ár lá.'*

---

* 'Our day will come.'

Bobby Sands
and the
Tragedy of Northern Ireland

John M. Feehan

Bobby Sands captured the imagination of the world when, despite predictions, he was elected a Member of Parliament to the British House of Commons while still on hunger-strike in the Northern Ireland concentration camp of Long Kesh.

* When he later died after sixty-six gruelling days of hunger he commanded more television, radio and newspaper coverage than the papal visits or royal weddings.

* What was the secret of this young man who set himself against the might of an empire and who became a microcosm of the whole Northern question and a moral catalyst for the Southern Irish conscience?

* In calm, restrained language John M. Feehan records the life of Bobby Sands with whom he had little sympathy in the beginning – though this was to change. At the same time he gives us an illuminating and crystal-clear account of the terrifying statelet of Northern Ireland today and of the fierce guerrilla warfare that is rapidly turning Northern Ireland into Britain's Vietnam.

THE TOM BARRY STORY
By Meda Ryan

The Tom Barry Story traces the career of one of Ireland's greatest guerrilla leaders during the War of Independence, his involvement on the Republican side during the Civil War and his rebellious attitude to the on-going conflict up until his death on 2 July 1980.

Tom Barry was always a controversial figure. There were those who thought 'there was no one like Tom Barry' — but there were others who said, 'he was an individual, a gift from God when wanted, but a bloody nuisance when he wasn't.'

THE DAN BREEN STORY
By Joseph G . Ambrose

Dan Breen was a guerrilla fighter and a revolutionary of the noblest tradition, dedicated to social as well as political change. He became a living legend in Ireland as one of the ablest and toughest soldiers in the fight for freedom.

BROTHER AGAINST BROTHER
By Liam Deasy

Brother Against Brother is a moving and sensitive account of the Civil War — one of Ireland's greatest tragedies. Liam Deasy tells in detail of the Republican disillusionment with the Truce, and later with the Treaty; how the Civil War began; how the Republicans were hopelessly outnumbered and hunted in the hills like wild animals before they were finally broken and defeated. He writes without bitterness or malice and gives us a rare and profound insight into the brutal and suicidal war that set father against son and brother against brother.